The Inner City in Context

The Final Report of the
Social Science Research Council
Inner Cities Working Party

The Inner City in Context

The Final Report of the
Social Science Research Council
Inner Cities Working Party

Edited by Peter Hall

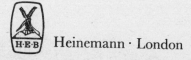
Heinemann · London

Heinemann Educational Books Ltd
22 Bedford Square, London WC1B 3HH

LONDON EDINBURGH MELBOURNE AUCKLAND
HONG KONG SINGAPORE KUALA LUMPUR NEW DELHI
IBADAN NAIROBI JOHANNESBURG
EXETER (NH) KINGSTON PORT OF SPAIN

British Library Cataloguing in Publication Data
The Inner city in context.
1. Metropolitan areas
I. Hall, Peter
307.7'6   HT167

ISBN 0 435 35717 4 (Cased)
ISBN 0 435 35718 2 (Paper)

Typeset by Castlefield Press of Northampton
Printed in Great Britain by
Biddles Ltd, Guildford, Surrey

Contents

Preface

This is the final report of the Social Science Research Council's Inner Cities Working Party, which met between October 1977 and November 1980 to fulfil its remit: 'to study the problem of the inner city in its temporal, spatial, socioeconomic, and policy context.' The objective was to make an introductory review of what was known about the inner city problem and of policy responses to it, with particular reference to Britain but within the wider framework of international experience; and in that light, to develop a programme of further original research on the inner city, that might be commissioned by S S R C.

To that end, the working party — whose names are listed immediately following this preface — appointed a research team working at the London School of Economics and Political Science under Derek Diamond. The members of this team, Stephen Kennett and Susan Laurence, produced research reviews which were intensively discussed at working party meetings, after which they were commonly further developed or otherwise amended. In addition, the working party and the team commissioned a series of specialist research reviews from outside specialists. These too were intensively discussed by the working party.

Most of the specialist reviews, and one or two of the more important papers by internal team members, were published in full by S S R C in March 1980, in the form of eleven separate reports; these are listed in the appendix of this book. The present book provides a capstone to the whole work, by digesting and synthesising the entire output of both internal and external reports, together with the working party's discussions of them.

In the event, as was only predictable, no individual working party member could possibly give his unconditional assent to every word of interpretation or judgement in the present text. If camels are horses designed by committees, the equivalent in publication terms is probably a dinosaur — and the report might well have taken as long as that creature took to emerge from its cave. To avoid that at all costs, the working party eventually left the drafting to its chairman.

The text, however, does reflect the work of many hands. To give credit where credit is individually due, and also to help the interested reader follow up the most important sources, the table of contents shows for each chapter a separate ascription of authorship — in every case save one chapter, either a member of the team or the chairman of the working party. Additionally, footnotes in the individual chapters show, where relevant, the particular published report (in the series of eleven) on which the material was based. Also shown, where relevant, are the most important of the external contractors' reports which fed into that chapter. Though of course direct quotations or lengthy summaries are cited in the text, it may be useful to realise that the general flavour of some reports has strongly infused individual chapters. A summary of the general argument of the book will be found in the second half of Chapter 1.

The final chapter sets out a programme of further work, which the working party felt to follow logically from the present state-of-the-art review. It was presented to the SSRC's Research Board in November 1979 and was finally approved by the Council in March 1980. Work on this further research programme is planned to start during 1981.

The working party would like to use this opportunity to thank the members of the research team — now dispersed — and the external contractors who made this work possible. They would also like to thank John Edwards, Angela Williams, Sheila Duncan and Gerda Loosemore-Reppen for their sterling services as successive secretaries to the working party. They also wish to acknowledge the work of Sally Burningham in her preliminary editing of the script before delivery to the publisher, and in searching for bibliographic references. Lastly, they would wish to acknowledge the financial aid of the Social Science Research Council, which provided the sole support for the project.

Peter Hall
Chairman, SSRC Inner Cities Working Party
London 1981

SSRC Inner Cities Working Party Membership

As at August 1980

Peter Hall, Professor of Geography, University of Reading (Chairman)

Gordon Cameron, Professor of Land Economy, University of Cambridge

Gordon Cherry, Professor of Urban and Regional Planning, University of Birmingham

*Derek Diamond, Reader in Geography with Special Reference to Regional Planning, London School of Economics

†H.J. Dyos, Professor of Urban History, University of Leicester

David Eversley, Senior Research Fellow, Policy Studies Institute

John Goddard, Professor of Regional Development Studies, University of Newcastle upon Tyne

Anne Lapping, Journalist, *The Economist*

‡R.E. Pahl, Professor of Sociology, University of Kent

‡Sandra Wallman, Senior Research Fellow, SSRC Research Unit on Ethnic Relations, University of Bristol

§ Peter Willmott, Director, Centre for Environmental Studies

Ken Young, Senior Research Fellow, Policy Studies Institute

Corresponding Members (from January 1979)

Peter Lloyd, Professor of Social Anthropology, University of Sussex

Bryan Roberts, Professor of Sociology, University of Manchester

Department of the Environment Assessors

Frank Gale

Michael Gahagan

Research Team

Stephen Kennett

Susan Laurence

SSRC Secretaries

John Edwards

Angela Williams

Sheila Duncan

Gerda Loosemore-Reppen

*Director, Research Team
†deceased
‡resigned, January 1979

‡resigned, January 1979
§ from May 1979

1 Introduction—Defining the Problem

Peter Hall

Is there a problem?

Of course Britain has an 'inner city problem'; that, surely, no student of the conventional wisdom would deny. After all, the newspapers and the television programmes have been obsessed with it. Successive governments since 1967 have launched programme after programme to try to deal with its various aspects. Waves of consultants have produced reams of reports on the subject. One government, in 1977, published a White Paper about the problem and then, the next year, passed an Act of Parliament to try to grapple with it. During the 1970s, resources were abstracted from the more prosperous parts of the country so as more effectively to fight the problem. So it must be real.

But is it? Looked at more closely, the so-called inner city problem is not one, but several problems. There is a state — which some label a problem — of demographic and industrial decline. There is a problem of concentrated poverty and deprivation. And underlying both, there is a problem of determining what kind of action — individual and collective, private and governmental — helped produce the present state of the cities, and what other kind of action might now change it.

Take the problem of decline first. London's population has fallen from a peak of 8.5 million in 1939 to less than 7 million at the end of the 1970s, with a projection of a further fall to as little as 6.5 million by 1991. Inner Liverpool had 700,000 people in 1921; by the end of the 1970s it had less than 300,000, with a recorded loss of 150,000 in the 1960s alone. The job losses have been, if anything, even more drastic. During the period 1961-71 London lost 243,000 jobs, inner Manchester 84,000, inner Glasgow close on 60,000, inner Liverpool 34,000. During the 1970s this loss accelerated: London alone lost 350,000 jobs between 1971 and 1979. And this loss has been differential: those who have gone have been disproportionately the professional and managerial classes and the skilled blue-collar workers, while those staying have tended to be the less skilled and the less affluent. Further, the arrivals have been dominated by Commonwealth immigrants, who — at any rate on arrival — tend to be mainly low-income people. And the job losses have been disproportionately concentrated in those sectors — manufacturing, transport, distribution — that formerly provided unskilled work for these lower-income groups (Davies 1978, 5–7).

Second, there is the problem of deprivation. Here, the figures seem stark enough. With 7 percent of the British population in the 1970s, the inner cities contain 14 percent of the unskilled workers, 20 percent of the households in housing stress, 33 percent of the Commonwealth immigrants, twice the national rate of unemployment, up to ten times the national proportion of people living below the Supplementary Benefit poverty line, up to four times the degree of domestic over-crowding found elsewhere in cities, over twice the national average of single-parent families, and less than half the national rate of car owner-ship (Kirby 1978, prelims). Though many — indeed most — poor people live outside inner cities on almost any possible definition, and many — indeed most — of those living in the inner city are not poor on usual definitions, nevertheless the annual income survey shows that the inner cities clearly contain an increasing proportion of all the deprived house-holds in the country.

Partly this is due to the character of the income support of the typical inner city resident: too many inner city workers are in unskilled work; too many, in consequence, are in jobs that are contracting or dis-appearing; too many are recent arrivals; too many are heads of large families, or are single parents, or are old-age pensioners. Too many therefore have a poor or insecure income base, or high outgoings, or both. More inner city residents than the national average live in sub-standard housing with poor amenities, especially in the residual private rental sector, but to some extent also in the older owner-occupied stock. Many appear to be pinned back in a vicious circle of poor jobs and poor housing through the joint operation of a technological-employment trap, whereby new technology allied to new economic organisation destroys their jobs and reduces their possibilities of finding new ones, and a housing trap, whereby they remain in rent-controlled private tenancies or in local authority housing, afraid to sacrifice their security and so unable to move to seek jobs that might well be available for them elsewhere. And this is compounded by the traditional poverty trap, whereby if they get better jobs they will lose more in taxation and loss of benefits than they stand to gain.

But these two syndromes are underlined by a third, that Lyn Davies calls collective deprivation (Davies 1978, 3). This is the additional loss that inner city dwellers feel because of their perception that opportunities fall short of what they need. It takes many forms: the physical deterioration of houses, factories, shops and streets; the lack of opportunities in jobs, housing, shopping, education and leisure; the poor level of many public services; and, underlying all this, the feeling that the whole area is just going downhill and that the most able and energetic and successful are leaving. Thus there is a deep sense that the people can no longer help themselves, that the sources of regeneration have failed, that all hope is lost — as manifested by a general feeling of alienation and apathy, demonstrated particularly at election times, but present constantly. And this perception is not limited to those who live there; it is shared by outsiders, who will not invest there. Thus the vicious circle of decay is intensified.

These three problem areas are clearly linked. Declining job opportunities exacerbate the deprivation of the unskilled inner city resident. Both in turn increase the collective sense of hopelessness and of alienation. In a vicious circle, this makes it even less likely that the inner city will contain energetic and thrusting entrepreneurs, or that it will attract capital from outside. Thus job prospects diminish again, and more people — again the more able and energetic — move out.

Critical Distinctions

One must still be careful to make distinctions and to ask critical questions when discussing these problems. Though they are linked, they are not identical with each other, and may have different origins and different possible remedies. As we shall see when we look briefly at history, in Chapter 7, the problem of inner city poverty and deprivation has long been with us. It was seen as a major question of the day in the 1880s, when inner city populations were still increasing through new arrivals from the countryside and from overseas, and when job opportunities — albeit in insecure, low-wage employment — were still rapidly expanding. Thus, while the recent shrinkage of employment may have exacerbated the problem, it certainly was not its origin. Similarly, then as now inner cities appeared as places of decay and despair, at least to outsiders; indeed more so than now, because of a population that was barely literate and had the most limited possibilities for independent political action. Looking at the problem the other way round, the recent sharp decline in inner city population and employment might equally well be regarded as a good thing rather than a bad thing. After all, deconcentration of our overcrowded conurbation cities has been in evidence for much of the twentieth century; and, since World War Two, it has become a major objective of British planning policy. Indeed, the new and expanded towns programmes that were created to fulfil this objective are generally regarded as one of the more conspicuous successes of the policy. If the process continues to roll on, why — so might an advocate of the new towns argue — should we suddenly object?

There is another critical reservation to make: by focusing too narrowly on something called an 'inner city problem' (or 'problems'), we may get a distorted perception of that problem. Consider for instance deprivation. We already noticed that a majority of inner city people are not poor, and that most of the poor live outside inner cities. So, if we link the terms 'inner city' and 'poor' — even in the loosest way, since no one believes that there is an exact correspondence — we make a false analysis and come to mistaken prescriptions. We run a real risk, for instance, of devising area-based policies that concentrate too exclusively on the inner city and thus help individuals or families that are in less need than individuals or families elsewhere. In fact, as we shall see in Chapters 3 and 6, there is a danger that this has already happened.

To avoid that here, we need to take the widest possible view. We need to take the central objective of our project to see *the inner city in context*. This means that we must first consider the inner city in the *spatial* context of the rapidly changing economic and social geography of contemporary Britain. In doing this, we are concerned not merely to document the trends, but also to explore what research has suggested might be the reasons for them. Then, we turn to the inner city in the context of the continuing debate about *poverty and deprivation* in Britain. Again, we ask what are the statistical facts, but again we try to go behind them, to the contributory causes as research has identified them. And in particular, we try to focus on the central question: to what extent are poverty and deprivation really concentrated in Britain's inner cities, and if so, why should that be so?

Then, after a brief diversion to look at the parallel American experience, we use that story to provide an introduction to the study of the inner city in its *political* or *governmental* context. We look at the policy responses of successive British governments to the so-called inner city problem. Following that, we turn to look at the inner city in its *historical* context. We briefly consider how far the so-called inner city problem has remained with us over time — at least over the past century. And at greater length we develop possible scenarios for the inner city in the medium-term future, assuming a dominant set of social and economic trends to which policy makers may respond in different ways.

Lastly, and springing directly from that analysis, we turn to the future, and look at the inner city in a *total research* context. We argue for a new kind of approach to the problem, and use insights from different social sciences in a combined attempt to understand the nature of the forces that shape the fate of the inner cities, now and in the future.

Presenting the Arguments

This book is deliberately short and — we hope — pithy. It tries to set out, with necessary supporting evidence but without excessive detail, the main line of argument that has emerged from the Inner Cities in Context project. Those who want such an overview should find it here. Those who want more detail should be able to find it in the eleven supporting volumes of research, listed in the appendix. The structure of this book follows the argument outlined earlier.

Chapter 2 views the British city in its *spatial* context. Taking up where the preceding international review left off, and setting the British economy within a context of rapid change within the world economy, it looks in more detail at the main demographic, economic and social trends in the entire British system of cities in the quarter-century after 1951. The central focus throughout is on the fortunes of the inner cities, but always as part of this total urban system. The chapter looks at the process of decentralisation out of the cities; asks how natural increase and migration help explain the process; examines the pattern of differential migration of socio-economic groups, to see whether social polarisation is affecting British cities; analyses in some detail the patterns of economic and employment change, with particular reference to the drastic contraction in manufacturing jobs and the apparent reduction in service jobs in many cities; and finally seeks to relate the flows of people and jobs, through a consideration of obstacles to mobility. Throughout this chapter, the emphasis is not merely on preserving and quantifying the trends, but equally on attempting to explain the forces that underly them.

Chapter 3 runs in parallel. It suggests that the trends in the previous chapter are not necessarily bad in themselves: the real problem seems to be one of relatively greater *poverty* or *deprivation* in the inner city than elsewhere, a problem that could be exacerbated by differential out-movement of particular socioeconomic groups. The critical questions are: first, who are the poor and deprived; secondly, why are they so; and thirdly, are they especially concentrated in the inner city? The most important findings are that poverty can indeed be explained largely in terms of occupation and personal circumstance; and that the problem does indeed appear to be somewhat more concentrated in large cities than elsewhere, though not to a very marked degree. In other words, though the degree of deprivation is greater in the inner cities than elsewhere, most people in the inner city are not poor or deprived on conventional measures, and the most poor or deprived people are found outside these inner city areas. So area-based anti-deprivation programmes should not provide the primary basis for an attack on deprivation, but rather should complement national programmes. Finally, the chapter emphasises a major theme that has emerged from work over the past decade: that deprivation is seen not so much as a matter of personal failings as a matter of external forces over which the individual or the household have little if any control.

Chapters 4 and 5 form an interlude — but, we hope, an important and useful one. Chapter 4 presents a very summary account of the evolution of the inner city in its spatial context *in the major industrialised countries of the world:* the United States, Europe and Japan. Drawing on recent research, it shows that down to the mid-1970s only the United States truly compared with Britain in the range and depth of its inner city problems. Though decentralisation and deconcentration were beginning to affect many other nations by that time, very seldom were they producing a major perceived problem of inner city decay. That, it suggests, may be because Britain and the United States were most advanced along a continuum of urban evolution, which might eventually lead other countries in the same direction. Thus, their experience might be uniquely valuable for urbanists and policy-makers in other nations.

Logically following from this. Chapter 5 turns to the *American experience* in more detail. It asks how far this is useful in understanding both the British inner city problem and the development of policy responses to it. It first looks at the strong tendencies in the United States toward inner city decline and metropolitan deconcentration since 1950, and above all since 1960. It emphasises particularly the changing spatial structure of the American economy, and what this has done for employment prospects in American cities. It examines the problem of poverty and deprivation in American inner city areas. Then, having established American parallels for the analyses made in Chapters 2 and 3 of this book, it looks forward to Chapter 6 and chronicles the

history of American policy responses to inner city decline and deprivation, from the mid-1960s onward. It reaches the disappointing conclusion that few of these measures have had much real impact on the
problem, which remains as stubbornly intractable as ever.

Against this sobering background, Chapter 6 looks at the evolution
of the British *policy response* towards the inner cities over the same
period. It shows how early responses were heavily influenced by the
American experience. This led, between the mid-1960s and the mid-
1970s, to a whole series of experiments in area-based programmes to
counter deprivation, usually in the form of compensatory social
provision to counteract what were seen as deficiencies in the local social
environment. It concludes that these policies were narrowly conceived,
though they may have had some useful outcomes. Then, in the mid-
1970s, came a major shift in thinking: deprivation was now seen as
arising from the workings of the socioeconomic system and could be
remedied therefore only by major changes in that system which would
eliminate the root causes of poverty. The chapter traces the influence
of this thinking through the important inner area studies of 1977,
through the White Paper of that year, to the Inner Urban Areas Act of
1978. It seeks to make some preliminary and highly tentative assessment of these policies, and outlines the most recent initiatives following the May 1979 General Election.

This evaluation provides a background for considering *future alternatives*. Chapter 7 draws on a number of recent exercises in future forecasting to ask what kind of world the inner cities of the 1980s and
1990s may have to fit into. It concludes that these forecasts are generally not very useful for this purpose, since they work on a global and
hence very coarse scale; but that their most usual common assumption
is of a rather constrained low-growth world, which is unlikely to be
very favourable for the inner city and its people. Starting from there,
the chapter poses a number of alternative economic futures for the
inner city, some of which appear rather more plausible than others. It
considers also whether social or technological changes could cause any
major disjuncture in the future position of the inner cities *vis-à-vis* the
rest of the urban system, and concludes that no very radical change is
likely. All in all, the chapter concludes on a moderately pessimistic
note: the problem, that has run like a theme throughout the book, is
that the inner city is caught up in powerful forces, especially of an
economic and social nature, that are working to its detriment.

This leads on logically to the final chapter, Chapter 8, which sets out
a *research agenda* for further work on the inner city in context. The
heart of the research programme is a comparative study of some local

urban economies, carefully chosen to range from the depressed and deprived to the thriving and prosperous; its aim would be to try to understand in detail the forces that bring decline to one city, and growth to another. Previous research, it is suggested, has focused too narrowly on decline; it is more important now to look at the less problematic places, to understand why they should be that way and to ask whether the problematic places could hope to emulate them.

Thus the present volume is only a staging-post in research on the inner city. It sets out what we think we know now — meaning by 'we' not merely the working party that commissioned the work, not merely the research team and the contractors who undertook it, but the whole wider research community whose findings and ideas have been extracted, summarised and synthesised here. It also, at the end of each chapter, tries to summarise what we do not know, so as to feed in to the research agenda of Chapter 8. It is thus a state-of-the-art review in a field where the art is in a state of constant and rapid change. Soon, doubtless, it will be out-of-date. But meanwhile, it may help to illuminate where we are now and where we should be going next.

2 The Inner City in Spatial Perspective

Stephen Kennett and Peter Hall

The Problem in Context

In many ways, this chapter forms the heart of the book. Its aim is to compare recent social and economic trends for different areas in Britain, concentrating on the special features of inner cities, but doing so by setting them within a wider context of change. Its stance is that there is agreement that a problem exists, but no agreement on its precise nature and causes; that precise definitions of terms like 'urban' and 'inner urban' are theoretically and practically difficult; and further, that these definitions have important implications for the ways in which issues are portrayed and policies are formulated.

Most important, the chapter tries to argue that the inner city problem — however delineated — can only be understood in relation to the wider metropolitan area within which its inner city lies, and to other metropolitan areas. The inner city is a part of this wider whole, and not a discrete part: it is a component of a hierarchically ordered, interactive and dynamic spatial system. To produce realistic policies for the inner city, we first need to understand its relationship with the wider urban area of which it is a part, and then with other cities in the regional and national hierarchy (Goddard and Spence 1976, 16). And we need to relate this to changing patterns of ownership and control of firms and industries.

We need however to go further: to understand the changing economic base of the city, as it is affected by rapid and fundamental shifts in the national and the world economy which affect its competitive position. We have to understand the changing geographical pattern of output of different goods and services, which depends on a rapidly changing composition of output, productivity, control, and technology of production and distribution. These changes are occurring both within the British space-economy, and between Britain and its international competitors — often to the detriment of Britain, and particularly of its weaker areas.

The aim, then, is to provide a synthesis of research that has studied the inner city in its urban and regional context, to describe the demographic and economic trends that operate within the system; and to try to delimit gaps in our understanding of these trends. In this way, hopefully, the relationship between social processes and spatial problems may be illuminated. Yet there is a danger here: by identifying an 'inner city' problem, we may perpetrate a myth that a whole range of social problems — unemployment, overcrowding, population decline — may be uniquely associated with the inner city. We need to determine whether there are attributes that are indeed unique to one set of areas, as against those that to some degree are found across the entire space economy. And to achieve that, we need detailed investigation of trends in other areas: urban, suburban, and rural, fast growing, slow growing, stagnating and declining. When this is done, invariably it is found that there are no features unique to some places: thus work on deprivation suggests that 'if inner cities are defined narrowly, then a large share of any given problem lies outside them' (Harrison and Whitehead, 1978, 34—5).

The initial difficulty, then, is that it may be misleading even to try to define 'inner areas' as such. Until the problems are properly defined, it may be dangerous to try to relate them to social and economic phenomena for a particular set of areas. Yet to achieve any advance, some framework of geographical analysis must be adopted. So, in much of the descriptive analysis that follows, a working definition of the inner city must be used. The resulting areas can be compared and contrasted both with each other and with other elements in the entire urban system.

Area Definition and Data[1]

To achieve our objective, two technical problems must first be addressed. The one is to produce the best possible — or more accurately, the least bad — working definition of the inner city in its wider spatial context. The other is to discover what kinds of information are available within the framework, and what pitfalls they present. Each issue will be briefly examined in turn.

Inner city definitions tend to have a chameleon-like nature. Most recent contributions to the debate, for mainly pragmatic reasons, have

[1] More detailed evidence for the issues being discussed in this subsection is presented in Eversley and Bonnerjea (1980), *The Inner City in Context*, Paper 2, principally 1—6 and Kennett (1980a), *The Inner City in Context*, Paper 7, principally 1—19.

adopted arbitrary and to some extent inconsistent definitions of the subject areas. But there have been at least three more systematic attempts at defining inner cities in relation to the rest of the country. The first divides the official Census conurbations into inner and outer parts; it is a useful starting-point, but it fails to take sufficient account of trends outside the conurbations. A second focuses on the planning regions or sub-regions. These latter provide straightforward comparison between the conurbations and the other parts of the country, but their boundaries are for the most part arbitrary, and the conurbations are not subdivided into inner and outer components.

Therefore, a whole body of recent literature has used a third approach which has aimed to define functional urban regions and/or labour market areas. The most popular definitions so far developed are the Metropolitan Economic Labour Area (MELA) and Standard Metropolitan Labour Area (SMLA). These are both derived from American work; and they embody the notion of a concentrated core of employment, surrounded by a ring or rings from which resident workers commute to the core. (The SMLA limits are formed by the zone from which at least fifteen percent of resident workers commute to the core: the MELA extends further to include the whole commuter field as long as more resident workers do not commute to another core) (Kennett 1980a, 9). MELAs and SMLAs are an invaluable aid for comparative analysis of trends within the wider urban framework, but in the context of this chapter — and of this book — they share with planning regions an important deficiency: their 'cores' are in most cases considerably larger than any reasonable definition of the inner area of the conurbation.

The problems of area definition are compounded by the problems of data: indeed, 'the end result can only be as good as the data' (Eversley and Bonnerjea 1980, 5). Most macro-studies naturally rely on published statistics which inevitably have limitations. The most important is that so much of the data are out of date: the 1971 Census has been updated only by surveys of narrower scope and less accuracy. Thus crucial recent changes in the space economy remain inadequately charted and understood. Nevertheless it is surprising that most researchers have not made more frequent use of such sources as the New Earnings Survey, the national Dwellings and Housing Survey, and the Office of Population Censuses and Surveys annual population estimates together with its vital statistics for local authority areas. This chapter will in part try to remedy that deficiency.

That is not of course to say that the Census, even when up to date, is without flaw. By its nature, it can provide only a 'snapshot' of a dynamic process. That can be partly overcome by inter-censal comparisons, but unfortunately major demographic shifts or economic cycles tend not to coincide with the census takers' decennia or quinquennia. And such comparisons are too often vitiated by changing criteria or definitions, or even by plain unreliability due to underenumeration or deficiencies in sampling — especially, for instance, in the 1966 sample Census. Further, an important area of economic activity is outside the scope of the Census: recent estimates suggest that anything between 5 and 25 percent of G D P, in advanced industrial economies like Britain's, may now come from the 'informal' or unenumerated sector of the economy, and in the inner city its importance could be much higher.

So the definitions will inevitably be arbitrary and the data less than perfect. But we will do the best we can. In the remainder of this chapter, we focus first on population trends over the period since 1951 — and in particular since 1966. We shall see that population decline has rapidly spread from the inner areas of conurbations, to most nineteenth-century towns. But, as metropolitan Britain has spatially expanded, this process of decline is contrasted with a parallel process of growth. Housing trends present a similar paradox: all nineteenth-century towns seem to have problems, but on the one hand they vary in intensity between one place and another, even between apparently similar places, while on the other the solution to the problems is partly provided by the development of new housing in the growth areas. Thus, in the search for explanation, population and housing changes cannot be understood merely in terms of a bundle of statistics for the inner cities; they require analysis of the dynamics of the entire spatial system, and of its relation to changes in life styles, developments in transport technology and other variables.

Attention then turns to changes in employment and industry. Again, the trends are seen to operate across the entire urban system: a focus on the declining areas will not completely explain the complex mechanisms of closure, opening, and relocation of plants. Equally, comparison of demand and supply for labour may aid description, but little more. In reality the causes of change lie in the decisions made by managers, and thus require a wider framework. Neither the small firm — so much vaunted as a solution of late — nor the growth of office employment, are seen as providing m ich potential succour for the inner city. The overwhelming influence is that of large multi-plant corporations and the decisions taken inside them — in particular, to close less efficient and more cramped inner city plants, and to open or expand high-productivity peripheral units, often with little employment gain.

Thus the trends, and their underlying causes, will be seen to be integrated both across geographical space — nationally and internationally — and across different fields of analysis and of policy. Trends in population, housing, employment, investment, planning, transport, education and social service provision form a complex web. To try to tease out some of the causal connections is a major aim of the remainder of this chapter.

Population trends[2]

Population trends since World War Two, and in particular the process of population redistribution, represent arguably the most fundamental force for change in the urban system. For, starting about 1951, a great reversal took place: the long-continued process of progressive urbanisation of the population that had been characteristic at least since the Industrial Revolution was replaced by a process of 'counter-urbanisation', in Brian Berry's term (Berry 1976, 8). Perhaps, then, for population trends the period 1951—71 may come to be seen as a great turning point in significance to those associated with the Industrial Revolution itself.

Within this section we therefore look at the principal trends. We employ a framework of Metropolitan Areas, recognising that the analysis does depend very much on the way the area boundaries are drawn; nevertheless these units are the best available. We focus particularly on cores of Metropolitan Economic Labour Areas in relation to the rest of the economy, and where possible we also try to distinguish separately the trends in the inner parts of these cores, especially in the major conurbations. The processes, to stress the point yet again, have to be comprehended across the entire space-economy; decline and growth must be seen as two sides of the same coin. But it will aid analysis first to distinguish the effects of natural growth and of migration; and then to study movements both within and between the local labour market areas, with special stress on the former.

Birth rates

Nationally, birth rates increased from the mid-1950s until 1964—5, after which they declined and at an increasing rate during the 1970s — until

[2]This sub-section was mainly drawn from the more detailed evidence presented in the literature review by Kennett (1980a), *The Inner City in Context*, Paper 7, principally 21—43, and the report by Eversley and Bonnerjea (1980), *The Inner City in Context*, Paper 2.

a very recent upward swing in 1978—9. This swing has so far only returned birth rates to their 1975 level. Thus, despite a much larger population, absolute numbers of live births are now currently less than in the mid-1930s. By contrast, death rates have changed relatively little for many years. So population increased substantially from the mid-1950s to the mid-1960s; more slowly in the late 1960s and early 1970s; and is now approximately static. These natural trends have been experienced virtually nationwide. For individual areas internal migration is a much more important component of population change and may swamp the perturbations in birth and death rates.

Labour markets

When we analyse the trends within and between the local labour markets (or the metropolitan areas), migration has been chiefly responsible for the overwhelming trend of decentralisation. Despite important differences from one city to another, it is generally true to say that for the urban system as a whole, populations of urban cores were static or still growing during the 1950s but began to decline during the 1960s. Initially, the growth areas were suburban ones — the rings of the SMLAs. More recently, much of the growth has transferred outside the SMLAs into the outer metropolitan rings of the MELAs — that is, towards the limits of the commuter field and even beyond. Collectively, the urban cores grew by some 500,000 people in the 1950s and lost about 750,000 in the 1960s, by which time losses — already evident in the very biggest cities in the 1950s had become very general. In contrast the ring of SMLAs experienced continuous growth, accommodating over four million people in the two decades (Table 2.1). Yet urban cores were not the only areas incurring loss. The rural areas, outside the MELA boundaries, declined in the 1950s, though this loss was halted in the 1960s.

The biggest conurbations, as already noted, began to decentralise earliest. Most of their core areas now house a smaller proportion of their total city regions than in the early 1950s. In the inner areas of the conurbations, the rate of decline has been even greater. Within the largest city regions it is the fringe areas that have grown most dramatically (Figure 2.1). Thus suburban or small-town environments have apparently proved highly attractive for many people. Moreover, although many of the really large urban renewal schemes have been suspended in the bleak economic climate of the late 1970s and early 1980s, population decline from the cities has continued. In sharp contrast, the few city systems that continued to centralise have tended to

Table 2.1 *Population Change by Urban Zone 1951–61; 1961–71; 1971–74*
Absolute (000s) and Percent

		1951–61	1961–71	1971–74[1]
Urban Cores				
Britain	Abs	500	-719	-459
	%	1.9	-2.7	-5.9
Million cities[2,3]	Abs	-363	-1199	-473
	%	-3.7	-9.0	-13.2
Rest of Britain	Abs	863	480	19
	%	6.9	3.5	0.3
Metropolitan Rings				
Britain	Abs	1708	2503	442
	%	13.6	17.5	8.6
Million cities	Abs	783	828	53
	%	10.2	13.1	2.3
Rest of Britain	Abs	925	1675	389
	%	16.4	21.0	13.2
Outer Metropolitan Rings				
Britain	Abs	245	788	292
	%	3.1	9.8	10.6
Million cities	Abs	101	220	49
	%	7.2	14.7	9.2
Rest of Britain	Abs	144	568	243
	%	2.2	8.6	10.9

[1] Ten year % rate of change.
[2] Million cities: MELAs with 1971 populations of over one million: London, Birmingham, Glasgow, Liverpool, Leeds, Manchester, Newcastle.
[3] Source: Kennett and Spence (1979), 220.

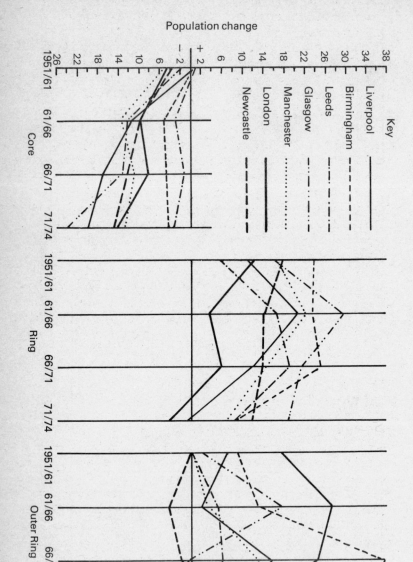

Population change

cluster in two areas — either adjacent to the conurbations, or in peripheral rural areas that are still experiencing the older tradition of movement off the land.

Our evidence after 1971 is less exact than for the 1960s; with the reorganisation of local government in 1974 it has been impossible to update city region or labour market data used in the rest of this analysis. Nevertheless population loss from the new Metropolitan Districts (or conurbation cities) has continued (Kennett and Spence 1979, 223), although it appears that the decline after 1971 was less severe than between 1966 and 1971, the period of maximum urban renewal. The pattern has not been geographically uniform: although in most cases there has been a roughly concentric pattern of the intensity of outward population shift, there have also been great variations from one conurbation to another. Thus at one extreme, the 'inner core' of Birmingham lost nearly a third of its population; while at another, in Tyne and Wear the 'core' of Newcastle declined less sharply than some of the outer areas of the metropolitan county.

Logically, this account concentrates on recent trends. But it needs emphasising that some of them represent only a continuation and an extension of trends over a much longer historical period. Inner London, as a whole, for instance, has been losing population since the turn of the century, with particularly drastic population losses during and immediately after World War Two.

Movement between

So far we have been emphasising the shifts of population within local labour markets. But as part of the same process, smaller — but still significant — numbers of people have been moving between these 'daily urban systems'. An important feature of population redistribution, in post-1945 Britain, has been the presence of a large number of such areas with persistently low growth or even decline. They are concentrated disproportionately within the Northern and Yorkshire-Humberside regions, and Scotland. Conversely the southern half of the country — with the anomalous exception of London, Bath, and the Rhondda — records almost ubiquitous growth. The so-called intermediate areas show a more varied picture; particularly important is Lancashire, where a pronounced decline in the 1950s was reversed in the 1960s through population decentralisation from the Manchester and Liverpool urban systems. The outer South East has continued to grow most rapidly in conjunction with contiguous areas in neighbouring regions (the South West and East Anglia). Many remote areas previously losing population to the cities are now growing quite rapidly, the most notable examples being northern Oxfordshire, Powys and Cornwall, and the eastern Highlands of Scotland (Kennett and Spence 1979, 223).

Net migration

These aggregate shifts can be attributed to variations in natural change or to net migration. But at the local scale it is the latter that is overwhelmingly important — as suggested earlier. With some exceptions (rapid natural increase in new and expanded towns, decreases in retirement resorts) natural increases do not show startling variations from one part of the country to another. In the past, large cities tended to be 'population factories', producing people for export to surrounding areas (Broadbent 1977, 100), while in the 1960s high rates of natural increase helped mask the rapid out-migration. But, with the national fall in birth rate reflected everywhere, this has ceased to be the case: because families tended to leave the cities early in their productive cycle, natural increase declined, if anything, rather earlier in the cities than elsewhere. The upturn in births in 1978 and 1979, conversely, seems particularly marked in the inner cities. Only about one third was due to a larger cohort of females entering the childbearing age; another one-third represented postponed births, and roughly one-third the impact of the differentially high fertility of mothers of New Commonwealth descent. This factor is particularly significant in some inner cities, especially London and Birmingham. And the age structure of these groups is now so different from the rest of the population that the phenomenon may well be a very temporary one.

Overall, indeed, the long-term prospect is of actual population decline. But a return to the national population level of forty million does not imply a return to the experience of 1911 (Eversley 1978, 8). As will later be seen, there would be many more households, an actual majority of which — the old, the unemployed, the one-parent families with one earner and several children — might be experiencing problems.

Since natural increase shows relatively little spatial variation, change has come about through the complex processes of migration. Mobility rates in Britain in recent decades have been about one in eight of the population per annum. Between 1966 and 1971, 17.5 million people — a figure equal to the combined populations of the major conurbations — are recorded as having moved at least once. After 1961, as already seen, there was a very marked out-migration from the inner areas of conurbations — and in London, from outer areas also. Most movements took place within city regions, from cores to rings or outer rings; but the larger cities: losses began to spill into neighbouring MELAs, thus producing local satellites (Kennett 1980a, 25). It must be remembered, though, that net movements are the result of much larger gross movements in both directions, often very finely balanced in amount but of very different character. Much of the countervailing inflow into the major cities came from more distant labour markets.

Class, Age, and Race[3]

Both inflows and outflows tend to be highly selective in terms of socioeconomic composition or of age. Generally, it is the richer, more dynamic, more self-sufficient who have left the inner areas for the rings. As decentralisation has progressed, the proportion of those in the upper socioeconomic groups in the cities has declined, while those with lower-than-average income, as well as the young adults and the relatively old (who indeed form many of the low-income groups) have proportionately risen. However, there has been some change in this pattern. While in the 1960s there was a marked out-movement of young adults and their young children, since 1971 there has been an increase in the younger adults and in the 5—14 age group. Some of this is explicable in terms of ethnic composition, but it has already had important effects on the projections of future school population, for instance.

While, generally, white-collar workers and their families have moved out faster than manual workers, in London there is also a strong in-movement of these white-collar groups, especially female professional workers. This is related to an age-group phenomenon: there has been a consistent flow of 15—24-year old single persons into the cities — in London heavily biased towards females — and an outflow of married people with young children. Indeed, the socioeconomic composition of the migration streams is heavily affected by age composition: many of the immigrants are students, apprentices, and junior workers, who will eventually rise in status and will fit into a higher socioeconomic group by the time they in their turn move out.

This indeed is a crucial point. While population changes largely result from migration, socioeconomic characteristics can just as well arise from social mobility *in situ* as from the differential migration patterns of various groups. Viewed statically, skilled manual workers form the largest single group of employed males; white-collar workers are some-

[3] This sub-section was mainly drawn from Kennett (1980a), *The Inner City in Context*, Paper 7, principally 50—96, and Eversley and Bonnerjea (1980, *The Inner City in Context*, Paper 2, 15—19 and 23—5.

what more concentrated in metropolitan rings than in either cores or outer rings. Conversely, outer rings have slightly higher proportions of manual workers, both skilled and less skilled, but the cores as a whole do not have radically different socioeconomic profiles from the national average. But the static point-of-time picture is less significant than the dynamics of socioeconomic change. During the 1960s — and presumably also the 1970s — Britain showed significant increases in managerial and professional, and intermediate non-manual groups, with commensurate decreases in the proportions of skilled, semi-skilled and unskilled manual groups. While the declines in the manual groups have been relatively ubiquitous, the increase in the higher status groups — though notable everywhere — has been most marked in the rings. Thus, though the managerial and professional groups have increased in the urban cores — indeed they are the only group to grow in these places — in *relative* terms this group has decentralised from cores to rings.

One result has been the increasing concern about the alleged phenomenon of social polarisation. Migration, it is argued, could bring about bi-polarisation, with an increase in both ends of the spectrum, and a decline in the middle, or alternatively uni-polarisation, whereby both the top and the middle people depart, leaving disproportionately the less skilled people behind in the cities. Both variants, it is argued, are most likely to occur in the biggest cities — and London, in particular, could become a city of the rich and the poor, as New York was alleged already to be. The analysis by Hamnett casts doubt on this, denying any significant effect of migration on the social structure of London (Hamnett 1976a, 270). However, his tabulations do not compare the relative changes in socioeconomic group distribution in inner London with the rest of the region, or the country as a whole, and therefore does not definitely remove this fear. Indeed, more recent work suggests that insofar as the data permit, bi-polarisation — and, in some cases, uni-polarisation — are indeed occurring in the inner areas of conurbations (Eversley and Bonnerjea 1980, 25). There is certainly room for much more research on this point. But, insofar as we have evidence, it does seem that social mobility of the labour force *in situ* is at least as important as migration. What is unclear is whether this internal restructuring arises primarily from pure social mobility of individuals, or from the net effect of entries into and exits from the labour force. Here, too, there is room for more analysis.

Not only has migration been differential in terms of its influence on age and on socioeconomic composition, it has also been highly specific in terms of ethnic group, causing specific concentrations in certain parts of certain inner cities. True, the picture here is distorted by lack of data — which the 1981 Census, shorn of crucial questions, will do little to remedy. What we do know is that only a handful of labour market areas, in 1971, had a non-British-born population amounting to ten percent or more — among which, London and Birmingham were especially prominent. By 1981 such figures have in any case become irrelevant, since a high proportion of the 'immigrant' population are British-born. Generally while immigrants from continental European countries and from the old Commonwealth tend to live in the better-off districts, especially in central London, those from the New Commonwealth tend to live in the ring between the central area and the outer boroughs: the classic 'inner city' location that contains a higher proportion of housing in poor condition than elsewhere (Gilje 1975, 18).

However, it is clear that the presence or absence of immigrants is not in itself a good indicator of the quality of the environment or of the prevalence of social problems. 'Difficult' areas such as Merseyside and Tyneside have few immigrants, while other areas with high proportions do not feature on the social priority lists — especially those in medium-sized cities such as Leicester. On the other hand, in many London boroughs as well as in Manchester and Birmingham, there is a high degree of congruence between proportions of ethnic minorities and deprivation.

For city regions as a whole no marked degree of ethnic segregation was observable in 1971; nor were there strong patterns of concentration within the subdivisions of metropolitan areas as used in this chapter. There is however some evidence of increasing segregation at the smaller grain ward level of some ethnic groups, for example Indians and Pakistanis. This is probably due in part to their strong community links and desire for owner-occupation, coupled with their low position on local authority housing lists. They have shown a tendency to concentrate in poorer-quality owner-occupied housing in the older parts of the core cities, as in the Small Heath area of Birmingham or the Manningham area of Bradford. But much of the *de facto* segregation here is at the very fine grained level, not caught by census statistics (Jones and McEvoy 1978, 165).

To summarise the most important demographic trends: broadly, but by no means entirely, the cities are characterised by population decline and the commuter rings by the most rapid growth rates. Losses and gains are the head and tail of the same dynamic. Superimposed on this feature are the complications caused by the geographical locality or the population size of the area. The discussion has also highlighted the great degree of hetereogeneity, not only between major cities, but also within them. The debates on social polarisation, and on the impact of migration, are very relevant here. If there are imbalances in some inner city areas, then almost certainly there are equal imbalances, less remarked upon, in other parts of the entire urban system. In essence then, it is dangerous to concentrate too exclusively on any single facet if one really wants an explanation of the totality of the processes.

The Motives for Migration[4]

Traditionally, academic studies of urban change have tended to postulate simple — and even simplistic — motives *a priori* for these trends. That is equally true of the Chicago sociologists' famous 'invasion and succession' model of the 1920s, as it is of more sophisticated modern econometric techniques (Bonnar 1976, 1). Nor will pure statistical associations tell us much about the real motives for movement, though they may provide suggestive leads — for instance the evidence that areas with relatively low turnover are characterised by predominantly British-born populations, and by relatively high proportions of owner-occupied or publicly-rented homes (Perman and Moore 1975, 10).

There is no substitute, then, for directly seeking to discover people's reasons for moving by a direct questionnaire approach. Evidence already available suggests that a majority of moves are short-distance and are made principally for housing reasons — above all the desire for a better home, but also because of compulsory purchase or being given notice, finding costs too high, or sharing a dwelling. A much smaller number move long distances — generally between regions — for work reasons. Thus, in the recent National Movers' Survey, some seventy-five percent of movers within London gave 'housing' as the chief reason, while more than fifty percent of those coming into London came for work reasons. In contrast, less than fifty percent of out-movers did so for 'work' or 'other than housing' reasons, though this is qualified by earlier work of Gould and Lacy (1973, 63—65) which suggested that a majority of movers from London to the rest of the South East no longer worked in London by the following year, so that most out-movers from London are in effect labour migrants whether the change of job and home occur simultaneously or not.

From such responses we can try to isolate some of the major forces

[4] This sub-section was in part drawn from the more detailed evidence presented in the literature review by Kennett (1980a) *The Inner City in Context*, paper 7, principally 46—50 and 82—83.

underlying the pattern of migration, beginning with *slum clearance and overspill policy*: this is a 'push' factor and it was very important in the 1960s, contributing to the dramatic loss of population in the inner parts of the great nineteenth-century cities. By the 1970s, with a reduction of national building programmes, demolitions were actually outstripping local authority construction in all but one of the provincial conurbations (Jones 1979, 207). Though comprehensive rehabilitation in the late 1970s may have had similar effects, it seems unlikely that the cities will ever suffer such dramatic losses again: there is too much land available in the cities, and overspill programmes have already been trimmed back.

Second, there is a 'pull' factor — *the desire for owner-occupation*. As living standards rise, families able and wanting to buy a home find poor opportunities in the predominantly nineteenth-century structures within inner areas, save for a minority of gentrifiers. The supply of new (or nearly new) owner-occupied housing, in relatively good condition, of the right size for family occupation, and at the right cost, is overwhelmingly at the periphery of the conurbation or beyond. But equally, many households have been excluded from the process because their incomes did not allow them to accumulate the capital for the down payment or to meet mortgage repayments — and it is these groups that have remained in the cities, sometimes in local authority housing with its notoriously poor mobility prospects, sometimes in low-quality privately rented housing. The only exceptions have been the new and expanded towns — to which areas migrants have overwhelmingly been motivated, like their owner-occupying equivalents, by the desire for better housing standards (Deakin and Ungerson 1977, 124).

Third, and associatedly, *the attractions of a suburban life style* — including not merely the physical ambience of a house with garden in a pleasant neighbourhood close to open country, but also the perceived attractions of what are seen as better schools and a higher social status. This life style has generally been restricted to those willing and able to pay the price of owner-occupation, though the publicly rented housing in the new towns has provided an exception for a small minority.

Shifting employment opportunities are a fourth factor. As already noted, employment is an important motivation for the minority of movers who do so over longer distances — though migration for retirement is also an important element. The problem is that it is very difficult to sort out the sequence of cause and effect in work-based migration. As we shall see, employment, like population, has shown net shifts

out of the conurbations, as has population — though here the process is
a complex one, dominated by plant closures and openings rather than
by actual movement. What evidence there is suggests that the net out-
movement of population began earlier than that for employment. Thus,
overall it is difficult to ascribe employment shifts as the cause for the
majority of workers — though it may have been so for a minority. An
alternative, as the evidence of Gould and Lacy (1973, 63-5) has already
suggested, is that out-movers may shift house and then almost immediately change their jobs. However, once these shifts have taken place the
new residential population immediately begins to build up a demand
for local services — and with these, new employment. Conversely, in the
areas of out-migration service employment will diminish. Thus migration of people must inevitably bring with it a considerable shift of employment — especially in the highly service-oriented British economy of
the 1970s.

Fifth, *developing transport technology* has played its part. In this
area, there have been particularly complex changes. Though in the
1950s and early 1960s it appeared that population was moving out of
cities — especially conurbation cities — earlier and faster than employment, since then the process seems to have got into better balance
(Gillespie 1980, 32—3; Kennett 1980a, 190). It is at least possible that
the earlier period was characterised by increasing separation of homes
and jobs, but that since then there has been a tendency to close up
again. Newer, lighter products tend increasingly to dominate in manufacturing industry, and these seek decentralised locations where labour
is more readily available. More recently, advances in information technology have permitted service industries too, to leave their traditional
city locations. At the same time, throughout both periods there was a
massive shift from public to private transport, associated with a massive
rise in car ownership: 58 percent of all households owned cars in 1979,
compared with 30 percent in 1961. Those who have left the cities have
tended to be those willing and able to commute by car — whether their
jobs are in the city or outside. But the process may have most unhappy
consequences for those left behind — which we shall need to take up in
a later section.

Housing[5]

As with so many other issues considered here, housing problems are not
just the result of housing market processes; and housing policy is only

[5]This subsection was mainly drawn from the more detailed evidence presented in
the literature review by Murie and Forrest (1980), *The Inner City in Context*,
Paper 10, and by Kennett (1980a), *The Inner City in Context*, Paper 7,
principally 213—42.

one strand of government action that may ameliorate — or exacerbate — those problems. So housing must not be artificially separated from all the other processes that affect the spatial organisation of activity: instead, housing questions must be discussed in the context of broad structural changes in the economy, that affect the position of different sectors and thus the life chances of the people in those areas where growing or declining firms are concentrated.

We start with a familiar lack of information. Little work on housing has been done within the framework of metropolitan areas. Though the 1977 National Dwelling and Housing Survey does allow us to associate housing conditions with the social and economic circumstances of the inhabitants, it does not yet allow us to conclude anything about changes in these relationships over time. So it is not easy to study housing within the dynamic, interrelated framework we have tried to use in this chapter. Nevertheless we can set out some facts.

The British housing stock is now relatively new compared with most countries except for those few like Germany, where war destroyed a high proportion of dwellings. The English Dwellings and Household Survey, in 1978, showed that by the end of 1977 there were 17.2 million dwellings — a net increase of over 1.2 million since the 1971 Census. Of a total 16.8 million households, just over one-quarter lived in pre-1919 dwellings, another quarter in inter-war dwellings, and just under half in post-war dwellings. By 1980 this last figure was estimated to be just over one half. And, by 1977, the dwellings which were in one was or another deficient in sanitary provision had fallen to a mere 8 per cent. This figure, which is similar to that for Britain as a whole, is in fact the lowest for any major industrial country. For the whole United Kingdom, nearly 10 million new dwellings have been created between 1945 and 1981; this represented close on half the total stock of 22 million at the latter date.

Dominant forms of tenure

This housing stock is increasingly dominated by only two forms of tenure: half the nation's dwellings are owner-occupied, one-third are rented from local authorities. Owner-occupation has burgeoned from just over one-quarter of all dwellings in England and Wales in 1947, to 55 percent by 1980; the proportion was rising by about 0.5 percent per year due to the volume of new private housing, plus — particularly after 1979 — council house sales. Further, this growth of owner-occupation has been as true of the older, pre-1914 housing as of the newer stock (Karn 1979, 160-90). However, there are considerable regional variations: owner-occupiership in 1971 ranged from 30 percent in Scotland to 58 percent in South West England. Publicly-rented housing varied, too, with the lowest ratios found in the North West and around London; privately-rented housing, nowhere currently very important, varies less. Nationally, new building for private rental has been minimal since the war. From 1960 to 1974 this sector declined by 36 percent, and since the Rent Act of that year the decline has been even more rapid. Thus, paradoxically, there has been a shrinking stock of housing available for occupation by those unwilling or unable to buy, while in the owner-occupied sector the high costs of buying and selling constitute a barrier to mobility, and the locally controlled public sector is notoriously unfavourable to new arrivals. Overall, therefore, there can be little doubt that the decline in privately-rented housing has constituted a powerful barrier to mobility.

As between individual cities and their commuter areas, owner-occupation tends to be highest in the West Midlands and lowest in London. But even in the inner conurbation areas the trend to owner-occupation was strong, with more than 50 percent of dwellings in this category by the mid-1970s (Karn 1979, 160-1). That represents a sharp change since 1971, when in all inner areas save Birmingham the public rented sector was more important. But there are variations in planning and housing policies.

In general, there are more people per room in inner areas than elsewhere, and more in public rented housing than in either privately-rented or owner-occupied dwellings. But this is as much due to differences in age structure, and to deliberate local authority allocation policies, as it is to financial status. In any case, there is sufficient variation to make it difficult to generalise about use of the stock, or about the relationships between housing condition and tenure. Consistently, the lowest densities of occupation are in the privately-rented sector where the elderly predominate, while the highest densities are in the newer council estates. High occupancy rates are also characteristic of owner-occupied housing in some inner cities — Manchester, Liverpool, and Birmingham — and appear particularly high where there are immigrant concentrations.

Post-War development

Broadly, the trend since World War Two has been for new house-building to reinforce the existing tenure patterns: places and areas with high proportions of publicly-rented housing (Yorkshire, the North, London) tend to have a good deal of new building in that sector, while areas having a high proportion of owner-occupied (the North West, the South East outside London) tend to concentrate housebuilding in that sector. Thus, while the proportion of owner-occupiership increased in all regions, so did the disparities between regions.

One major change has been the marked improvement in housing conditions since 1966. Sharing of dwellings fell sharply — and this was true even of Greater London, the area where sharing was and is more prevalent, partly because of its association with privately-rented housing in the central boroughs. Yet despite the continued existence of overcrowding and shared dwellings, there has been an increase in vacant dwellings — from 36,000 to 100,000 between 1961 and 1971 in London alone, or from 1.6 to 3.8 percent. (In inner areas as a whole the increase was from 4 to 8 percent.) Under-occupation, a phenomenon of middle-aged and older people who stay in their homes after children have gone, is in contrast, more concentrated in suburban rings: in inner areas, space tends to be too scarce and expensive to go under-used (Crofton 1975, 73).

Slum clearance, plus rehabilitation with improvement grants, have brought about a marked improvement in the condition of the housing stock. Yet in 1977 more than 1.4 million dwellings, structurally in sound condition, still lacked one or more basic amenities. And again there remain substantial differences between regions and cities, with the inner cities markedly worse than the rest. Big improvements have occurred during the 1970s, but lack of amenities, as well as overcrowding, is now very localised. Holtermann's work, based on 1971 Census data, reveals very big differences between conurbations: overcrowding tends to be worst in London, lack of amenities worst in the north, while only Central Clydeside does poorly on virtually every kind of indicator (Holtermann 1975, 40-1).

One aspect of housing improvement, however, could bring with it further problems. The phenomenon of bi-polarisation, discussed earlier, indicates the extent of gentrification of the housing stock in certain areas. Admittedly, evidence for both the location and the scale of gentrification is lacking, even in London. It is probably not easy to catch at the scale of the inner city or even at the level of the urban ward; rather, it is to be seen down at the level of the neighbourhood or estate. In such gentrifying areas, there will be households at different stages of their housing careers: long-established, elderly working-class owners will be living alongside younger, professional householders climbing on to the housing ladder for the first time, giving a social mix — at least for a short period. Progressively — and, perhaps, more rapidly in the 1970s than in the 1960s — urban areas tended to become more segregated at the very local scale; some parts becoming privileged localities, others concentrations of those who lack the resources and the opportunity to move. True, the evidence does not suggest that a majority of the deprived are yet concentrated into such depressed areas. But the trend seems to be slowly but surely in that direction.

Thus housing problems do remain to plague some regions and some cities. Though the crude number of dwellings roughly equals the number of households, shortages persist. Despite the dramatic decrease in London's population in the 1960s, overcrowding actually declined there less rapidly than elsewhere. Partly, this reflects the effect of slum clearance. Between 1971 and 1977, overcrowding nationally was further reduced: the percentage of households living at densities of over 1.5 per room fell by two-thirds, and of those living at between 1 and 1.5 per room by nearly two-fifths. But overcrowding was more prevalent in London. Nationally, by the latter date. only 3 percent of households lived at 1 or more per room, but 8 London boroughs — a quarter of the total — had more than 5 percent of households in this category. This residual overcrowding cannot be ascribed to slum clearance or to the home improvement policies developed after 1969; it is doubtful indeed whether it is due even in part to gentrification. Outside London, it is notable that some of the districts with the worst overcrowding — in Bradford, Liverpool, Manchester and Kirklees — have no history of gentrification, while only in Liverpool has there been major demolition. The common factor seems to be high concentrations of households descended from Commonwealth immigrants — but it would be wrong to say that they were overcrowded because of slum clearance or improvement grants. The evidence does not support simple generalisations that blame particular policies, or particular authorites, for the residual overcrowding problem. Between 1955 and 1979, some 1.7 million houses were demolished or closed in Britain, and — in England and Wales alone — some 3 million people were rehoused. Similar effects have resulted from improvement policies, especially after 1971.

Yet another important factor in the housing equation, and indeed one of the more striking social facts about the post-World War Two era, has been the rapid growth in the number of households relative to population. This has been particularly true of the 1970s, when — despite a stagnant or declining population — households increased and average household size fell, from 3.09 in 1961 to 2.89 in 1971 and 2.67 in 1979. There are many contributory factors: the falling birth rate, with fewer children per family and many more childless families; the increasing numbers of old-people who live alone; the tendency for teenage children to leave the parental home earlier to set up households of their own; and the rapidly increasing divorce rate, creating two households out of one. Further, household formation is related to availability of housing. If supply increases, young couples and individuals are more likely to establish households of their own, and both sharing of dwellings and multi-occupation of houses will decline. Thus it may be argued that the housing problem is one of fit rather than shortage (Vale 1971, 5).

Crucial questions

What is clear is that the crude arithmetic of supply and demand is not sufficient: the crucial questions are not about numbers of dwellings, but about where they are and whose needs they do or could meet. These questions are closely related to the question of tenure, which in turn is associated with socioeconomic group and income. Owner-occupiers tend to be drawn from the non-manual, higher-income groups, council renters from manual occupations — especially skilled ones. Furnished private tenancies tend to cater for a more diverse range, including young professional couples and individuals willing to pay a relatively high rent, as well as transient socially disadvantaged people unable to gain access to the more favoured tenures (Shepherd, Westaway and Lee 1974, 40). The point is that households tend to move within tenures rather than between them, and that lower-income (and older) households move less often — thus reinforcing the pattern of a dual housing market. But London, with its high rates of migration in and out, has a very special set of housing markets with quite unique problems requiring, perhaps, unique policy solutions (Johnson, Salt, and Wood 1974, 97). Though only 10 percent of London's households were in privately-rented furnished dwellings in 1971, this sector accounted for almost half London's overcrowded households (Shepherd, Westaway and Lee 1974, 44). The furnished sector has diminished greatly since then, and undoubtedly so has the amount of overcrowding found there. But it is still true that the highest rates of overcrowding include large families and groups such as unmarried mothers and non-white immigrants, who have special difficulties in gaining access to the more favoured sectors. However, it should be stressed that severe overcrowding occurs in only localised districts within inner London — and that East or South London demonstrate very little overcrowding at all.

In theory, it might be supposed that the continued out-movement of people and of jobs could only be beneficial. The inner areas enjoy lower densities, while the out-movers enjoy largely new housing, often at lower real cost than in the cities, even if this is to some extent offset by higher travel costs for some. Yet obsolescence in the inner cities has been compounded by the lack of investment — save perhaps in the London gentrification areas. Increased pressure from new, young arrivals, and from the better-off — especially in London — has maintained the pressure on the housing stock and made it more difficult for the poorly-housed to benefit from upward filtering (Webster 1978, 16). The public sector stock has obsolesced more quickly than might be expected from its age structure, because of unsuitable and unpopular kinds of building that the inhabitants treat badly. Moreover, Webster argues, there have even been problems in the areas of growth outside the conurbations — mismatch of labour demand and supply due to the smaller size of the local labour market, plus a shortage of privately-rented housing and rigid allocation rules for public housing which together hinder labour mobility (Webster 1978, 17). But, while these conclusions appear intuitively reasonable, there is little empirical work to support them.

This underlines the central conclusions about housing: that there is very little work relating the whole problem to broader shifts in the space economy, including the impact of demographic trends, the pattern of migration, the relationship between household formation and growth, and the financial burden of housing. The limited work that has been done, precisely because it concentrates too narrowly on the inner city as such, cannot illuminate these more basic questions.

In any event, the nature of the housing problem — and of policy responses to it — is changing radically. Government policies are working systematically to make housing a commodity for sale in the market according to ability and willingness to pay, rather than a service provided according to need. The future seems likely to consist of a nearly non-existent privately rented sector (except in London), a shrinking publicly-rented sector and a rapidly expanding — and quite dominant — owner-occupied sector. This picture could be altered by a growth of the 'fourth sector', of housing associations and similar housing, but overall this seems unlikely. Partly as a result of these changes, the quality of housing is no longer tenure-specific: it is no longer just the private tenant who has the worst housing, for increasingly there are bad council flats and bad owner-occupied housing too. In the council sector, only the worst dwellings in the least desirable locations — often, though not exclusively, in the inner city — are available even in the medium term. And a number of factors — among which the sale of council housing is only one — are working to make the local authority sector the residual one, providing for households with least choice. Equally, marginal owner-occupiers may find themselves fighting a losing battle with obsolescence and decay. Thus, while clearly those with the least resources have the least housing choice, their location is no longer tenure-specific to the inner city: pockets of physical decay, and concentrations of houses with least choice, exist in all tenures and in all parts of the city.

Taking all these factors into account, it is still difficult to understand why the massive housing effort of the 1960s and early 1970s has still left so many households in sub-standard dwellings, or sharing accommodation, or even homeless. Vacancies are one factor, but the 1977 survey put only 4 percent of all dwellings into the vacant or second home category, the same proportion as in 1971; that may however be an underestimate.

Nevertheless, Londoners seem to experience special problems. Increasingly, their housing market is invaded by wealthy expatriates who regard London property as a means of secure investment rather than as a means of shelter. Competition for housing space from tourists and other short-stay visitors, people buying second homes, company-owned executive flats, housing for foreign diplomats, and large numbers of students, all exacerbate the shortage. Thus dwellings are artificially withdrawn from the stock effectively available for London residents.

More important than this loss, and a national rather than a London phenomenon, is household fission — the process, already noticed, whereby more and more single people, together with the elderly and small groups of unmarried people, form separate households. Between 1971 and 1977 dwellings rose nearly 8 percent and population by only 0.6 percent — but households increased by over 6 percent, so that the improvement in housing standards was less than might have been supposed. Yet during this period, the number of multi-person households sharing dwellings dropped by a half, and of one-person sharing households by 20 percent; while 'concealed' households — married couples and lone parents sharing with parents or children respectively — fell by 35 percent. The problem is that while some areas now have a housing surplus, others — notably London and other areas with concentrations of immigrant-descended households — still have shortages and poor conditions for many, which show little sign of abating. At the same time, marginal Londoners — like marginal Mancunians and marginal Liverpudlians — find that both owner-occupied housing and public housing (alike in the local authority and housing association subdivisions) are allocated only to those judged conventionally acceptable. Once stray outside these categories, in terms of income or lifestyle, and the consequences in terms of housing can be dire.

Employment and Industry[6]

The shifting pattern of employment, clearly, is one of the root changes in the urban system. Indeed, though we chose to start with the symptom of population shifts and work through to employment, we could with equally sound logic have approached the question the other way round. Here, we consider the main facts of changing employment and industrial patterns, both sectorally and spatially. Later, we go on to see in some detail how a considerable volume of contemporary research tries to explain these trends.

Changes in the pattern of employment

The entire labour force of Great Britain grew between 1971 and 1978 from 24.8 to 26.3 million, both figures including unemployed. The outstanding feature of this period was that both employment and unemployment were growing. As in the 1950s and 1960s, the great bulk of the increase in employment up to 1978 was in jobs for women; male jobs in contrast grew very slowly indeed in the 1950s, and contracted thereafter.

This is associated with profound structural shifts. There have been substantial declines in employment in primary industries (agriculture, mining), a mixture of growth and decline in manufacturing, and — until recently at least — substantial growth in services, especially finance, distribution, education, and professional services. This growth in services continued strongly into the 1970s, in every region of the country; and it was dominated by an increase in female jobs, though this sector also saw some increase in male jobs. The most recent evidence suggests that in the late 1970s female employment growth, too, was slackening as new service industry jobs were balanced by disappearing factory jobs (Harris and Taylor 1978, 18). There must in any case be a limit: by the late 1970s the British economy was highly 'tertiarised', and the impact of labour-saving devices could be substantial in the near future.

These changes have not occurred equally across the British space-

[6]This subsection was mainly drawn from the more detailed evidence presented in the literature review by Kennett (1980a), *The Inner City in Context*, Paper 7, principally 97–161, and Goddard and Thwaites (1980), *The Inner City in Context*, Paper 4.

economy. Employment has traditionally been more concentrated than population: in 1971, more than 58 percent of jobs were in the urban cores, against only 48 percent of resident population. But while during the 1950s the cores marginally increased in employment, by the 1960s they were contracting as economic crisis was followed by shedding of labour. Many rural areas, still depending on farm jobs, also suffered losses in both decades. The most rapid gains were in the metropolitan rings, where the 15 percent growth in the 1960s was three times the national rate. The outer MELA rings declined in the 1950s, grew in the early 1960s, but then declined again in the late 1960s; so that the outward movement of people was certainly earlier and more pronounced than that of jobs.

In greater detail, it can be seen that declines affected progressively more and more — though not all — of the major cities. For London's core, a 130,000 growth in the 1950s turned into a 387,000 decline in the 1960s. Conversely, jobs in new and expanding towns grew rapidly. All this, it must be recalled, was fully in accord with the planning policies of the time. The outward shift of jobs from the largest cities often overlapped their rings and outer rings, passing into neighbouring metropolitan areas; thus, by the end of the period, larger MELAs tended to be losing employment overall. But superimposed on all this was a regional effect — with the South East and the Midlands growing faster than average, Yorkshire-Humberside and the North West and Scotland growing more slowly. Overall, however, the conurbations tended to be suffering faster employment losses than the rest of the regions in which they were located: the fastest-growing zones were the rings (and outer rings) around them, and neighbouring metropolitan areas (including new town MELAs). This was most marked in the 1960s, and above all in the second half of that decade, as national employment contracted.

Female employment

The conurbation cities have traditionally had more women in employment than other places, and during the 1960s some major cities with large job losses were actually increasing their female employment — not of course due to direct substitution, but because of declines in some sectors (especially manufacturing) and gains in others (services). The new female jobs have largely gone to married women, and many of them have been part-time. Further, areas that traditionally had fewest women in the labour force (for instance Clydeside) recorded the biggest increases. These profound changes result from complex factors including the decline in family size, the changing perceptions towards female work, and the upward socioeconomic mobility within the entire system — but these trends are insufficiently researched.

Service and manufacturing employment

The decline of inner city employment — as well as the countervailing increase in women's employment even there — reflects very large structural changes. Since 1966 all kinds of manufacturing jobs, with the sole exception of chemicals, have been declining in the urban cores. Among services, insurance, banking and finance, business and professional services, and public administration continued to increase into the 1970s. But the growth of service jobs failed to compensate for the decline in manufacturing ones and, further, the service increases took place at the higher managerial levels, while the more routine clerical jobs have also been contracting. Conversely, metropolitan rings have shown rapid increases in service employment, including the more routine jobs; and even the nationally-declining factory industries performed less badly there than elsewhere.

An outstanding trend is the dispersal of manufacturing jobs from the conurbation cores to peripheral regions and to small — or, more accurately, medium-sized — towns in less industrialised regions. These have benefited from good access to labour supplies, due to the decline in the local agricultural labour force, and from the residential preferences of technical and managerial workers for life in smaller towns and in rural areas (the previous indigenous industrial structure of the region appears to have been relatively unimportant). But such gains largely occurred in the southern half of England. Elsewhere, especially in male employment, manufacturing jobs declined and the growth of service jobs has not kept pace — partly because these areas have failed to attract service industry, partly because the industries that existed or have moved to these areas have not kept up with the national increases in these kinds of employment (Frost and Spence 1978, 46).

Latest developments

In the 1970s a change occurred. Though the loss of manufacturing jobs continued and even intensified — the six major conurbations accounted for 69 percent of the net national loss of manufacturing jobs — the growth, in percentage terms, was now quite diffused throughout what had previously been mainly rural or only partially industrialised counties. These form a broad contiguous belt from the South Coast in east Dorset and Hampshire, taking in part of the South West region

(Avon and Wiltshire), the western and northern sectors of the Outer Metropolitan Area and the Outer South East, with a spur running south of London to the Crawley-Burgess Hill area of Sussex, and thence to East Anglia and the northern part of the East Midlands region. Even here there are pockets of decline — the car-making centres of Luton and Oxford — but in general the picture is one of strong attraction to manufacturing, even in the period of tight industrial development control, which had been virtually abandoned by the end of the 1970s. Particularly strong centres are north Buckinghamshire (Milton Keynes) and that part of the East Anglia and East Midlands region running along the Cambridge-Peterborough axis. But even outside this favoured belt, there were gains in employment in more distant rural areas where previously there had been little industry: Northumberland, North Wales, the Highlands of Scotland (Keeble 1980, 947; Fothergill and Gudgin 1979, 195-6, 199-200). True, many of these regions were close to major metropolitan areas and were presumably receiving their overspill; true also, the absolute gains were much larger in the more densely settled areas. But there was no mistaking the direction of the change — and, since so much of the growth took place outside the Special Development Areas, it did represent a massive paradox for regional policy over the preceeding quarter century.

The South East

Overall, however, when service industry is taken into account we find that even in times of vigorous regional policy, it was the South East outside Greater London — together with immediately adjacent areas — that showed the fastest growth of the most rapidly expanding industries and occupations. The South East not only predominates in high-status jobs, but increasingly so. Though research so far has not linked this fact to migration trends, it seems plausible that it is in these occupations that people are willing to migrate for work reasons, while growth in clerical or manual employment is more likely to be filled by indigenous people having the right skills. So the areas of employment loss, above all from the cities, are unlikely to see out-movement of their lesser-skilled workers — and unemployment is likely to be the result.

Much of the service industry growth has of course been in office jobs — and office jobs have also increased in the manufacturing sector, as shopfloor jobs have declined. By 1971, more than 25 percent of total employment was in offices — of which 60 percent was clerical, 15 percent managerial, and 12 percent professional. But it is simply not true that office jobs have an affinity for major cities. With the outstanding exception of London, major centres actually have less office jobs than would be expected from their size. Further, the decline in manufacturing jobs in the conurbation cities has not been matched by an increase in office employment — for, as already seen, routine clerical jobs have tended to contract there. Office jobs have grown particularly rapidly in metropolitan rings and outer rings, and in smaller cores. Very often, this growth is in population-oriented service industries, including public sector jobs.

Indeed, the big conurbation cities have been relatively declining as office centres. During 1966—71 London, Birmingham, Manchester, Liverpool, Sheffield, Leeds, and Glasgow all recorded 'negative differential shifts' for the office sector, meaning that office employment there grew less rapidly than would be expected from their share at the start of the period. Government policies, in the form of the Office Development Permit system, working through the Location of Offices Bureau, contributed to this in London but not in the other cities, where the decline was spontaneous; even in London it might have occurred anyway. Conversely, medium-sized towns in the South East showed significant positive shifts. In other words, office jobs were decentralising to smaller places outside London's outermost commuter ring. Moreover in the provincial cities the structure of office employment is different from the national structure, with a greater proportion in routine clerical jobs, yet these have showed the lowest growth of all kinds of office employment and are the most vulnerable to technical change in the near future.

London, in contrast, had an economically favourable structure of office employment, with more people in the fast-growing managerial and professional jobs. Yet the favourable structure was outweighed by the differential movement of these same jobs, which took them to other towns in the South East, rather than to provincial conurbation cities. Indeed, less than fifteen percent of decentralisation from London actually left the South East. This minority long-distance movement mainly consisted of routine clerical work for which communication costs were low (Goddard 1978, 40—1, 45). In fact, as a whole the peripheral regions were losing office jobs at an increasing rate to the South East — above all in the most remote regions: Wales, the Northern Region, and Scotland (Burrows 1973, 25, 28). The higher-level control jobs, it appears, were staying in London and were even growing there. Thus London may be becoming richer and more powerful even while it becomes smaller.

We can now try to sum up the main trends. Everywhere, primary employment has been in decline. Everywhere, there has been a powerful trend for both manufacturing and routine clerical employment to move away from the big conurbation cities. This is only partially offset by a tendency for service jobs to locate nearby, within these same conurbations. Thus urban cores lost both manufacturing and lower level services, while other areas — mainly in those same conurbations — scored gains in both. In particular, there is a tendency for the most skilled, fastest-growing aspects of employment to be attracted to comparatively rural areas such as East Anglia, North Wales, Northern Ireland, and the Scottish Highlands. Such are the main facts. We must now go behind them, and try to summarise and synthesise a very considerable body of recent literature that seeks to explain them.

Components of change[7]

First, a caveat: most of the analyses described in the following pages work by trying to explain employment change. This is simply because the other kinds of economic measurement — like output or productivity — are not available at the fine-grained spatial scale we need to use here. It is clear that nationally, output has grown quite rapidly throughout the post-World War Two period, even while employment was growing slowly or declining. There have presumably been big variations by industry and by locality, but — apart from some relatively coarse generalisations derived from the Censuses of Production — we cannot draw any useful conclusions.

The first, and in many ways the most fruitful kind of analysis so far, consists in dividing employment trends up into their component parts: plant births, plant deaths, in-movements, out-movements, and *in situ* expansion or contraction of plants. Broadly, the results agree that births and deaths of firms or plants are a far more important influence on local employment changes than movements. In particular, inner cities suffer from a high rate of closures and — in some cases, though the evidence here is conflicting — from a lack of births of new firms or plants. Further comparative studies of cores and rings suggest that it is variations in the birth rates of plants that have mainly caused the net outward shift of jobs (Cameron, 1973, 134—6).

Components-of-change analysis also permits estimation of those sectors that are most likely to stay in inner cities, and those most likely

[7]This subsection was mainly drawn from the more detailed evidence presented in the literature review by Kennett (1980a) *The Inner City in Context*, Paper 7, principally 166—71.

to leave. Within Liverpool and Manchester, almost every major sector of employment is in decline, though the rates vary from sector to sector. In Clydeside only one out of eighteen sectors (leather and fur products) continued to centralise. This may suggest to planners that their inducements should concentrate on those sectors most likely to stay — or, more accurately, least likely to leave. But further, the analysis can be usefully disaggregated by firm size, firm type (single-plant or multi-plant), and plant status. The results vary surprisingly from one city to another. Manchester for instance is well endowed with small firms, yet no less than 20 percent of the employment contraction in its inner city was due to the decline of only 11 factories (Dicken and Lloyd 1979, 39). Merseyside's inner area in contrast has four-fifths of its employment concentrated in multi-plant firms.

Concentration of capital[8]

If there is such a degree of concentration of ownership, then presumably the inner city economy will be highly affected by changes in it — so logically we should turn to look at changes in plant ownership and especially the pattern of acquisition by firms of other firms. This reveals that while the acquired companies tend to be dispersed, the firms taking over tend to be concentrated. In particular, companies in peripheral regions appear relatively vulnerable to take-over by companies from the South East. The South East contains the most active acquirers, and has the greatest diversity of acquiring firms in terms of industrial sector. Top-level decision-making thus gravitates to the South East, while middle-management functions remain with the acquired firm: the South East becomes more and more a head office and control region, but with a low rate of factory expansion (Leigh and North 1978, 244). In contrast, peripheral regions have relatively few acquiring firms, and rarely take over firms in the South East.

The process of take-over affects both intermediate regions (like the Midlands) and really peripheral regions (like the North). But the first arises mainly through differential growth rates, while the second arises from differential acquisition rates (Goddard and Smith 1978, 1,084). The net result of these trends is that provincial cities find their manufacturing base increasingly controlled by non-local enterprises. As a result, they lose independent innovative capacity. That conclusion is fortified by the fact that in relation to population size, their admini-

---

[8] This subsection was mainly drawn from the more detailed evidence presented in the literature review by Kennett (1980a), *The Inner City in Context*, Paper 7, principally 149–51.

strative employment is relatively weak. The beneficiaries, again, seem to be the medium-sized urban systems around London. From the very limited evidence so far, it appears that there are significant differences between provincial cities: Merseyside for instance has a much higher level of external control than Manchester. Yet, though Manchester has a higher proportion of newer, smaller firms, it appears that prospects for growth based on local innovation are limited in both cities; many of the smaller firms fail to survive (Dicken and Lloyd 1979, 48–50).

Little research then has so far been done on these processes. However, it does appear that the acquiring firms are often (though not always) less efficient and proportionately less profitable than the firms they take over. Successful, growing firms seem particularly prone to take-over because they allow the bigger firms to extend their markets and acquire rival brand names. After take-over it appears that a higher-than-expected proportion of firms are closed, run down, or suffer restructuring with employment loss (Smith, I.J. 1979, 435–6). These findings appear to run contrary to those of other work. Leigh and North, for instance, found that acquisition was commonly followed by expansion of output, rather than by closure, due to an injection of investment plus better management; it could be presumed that even if there were productivity gains, employment would hardly contract in these circumstances (Leigh and North 1978, 240). But, if Smith's findings are generally true, the process of acquisition is likely to run directly counter to the notion that the small indigenous firm can generate substantial employment gains – though, possibly, increased employment may occur in other kinds of job such as offices, and in other plants owned by the acquiring company.

This conclusion is reinforced by the important work of Massey and Meegan (1979) on the restructuring process in the electrical engineering and electronics industry. Firms tend to restructure, they suggest, for three motives: to cut capacity and cut costs; to achieve scale advantages; and to improve market share. Older congested, badly laid-out inner city plants tend to be prime targets for closure. The results for typical big cities (London, Birmingham, Liverpool) are big losses either through closure, or the introduction of labour-saving techniques and methods, or through transfer of production to an existing or new site with reduced labour inputs. The most drastic effects came from concentration of production on other sites in order to reduce capacity and cut costs, where the recipients are generally medium-sized freestanding towns in semi-rural areas such as Lincoln and Rugby.

However, it would be misleading to generalise too far from a study of one industry over a short period of time. Even in this particular industry, the position by the early 1980s is that the biggest firms are in a relatively strong position. By their take-over policy they may have created local unemployment in the cities and in the development regions, but they have created employment elsewhere, in the places where efficiency considerations and managerial preferences coincided. There is a conflict of interest here between the efficiency of the national economy and the welfare of the urban economy in the older conurbations. Thus, whether or not restructuring involves take-over, the results appear the same: since the cities lose more jobs than the small towns gain there is a net reduction in employment overall, concentrated in the inner city location. Further, though the evidence is not conclusive, it appears that the biggest job losses may be among skilled workers, who – even if they find alternative employment locally – are likely to find themselves demoted to the ranks of the semi-skilled or unskilled. Conversely, the relatively few new jobs created elsewhere are likely to be unskilled, and to attract cheap, unorganised, surplus female labour (Massey 1976, 9; Massey and Meegan 1978, 287). And this is likely to be equally true, whether the extra jobs are created in assisted areas or in small towns with no special status. Though for example Keeble (1976, 287–8), among others, has concluded that Assisted Area status has been important in job creation in peripheral regions, Massey suggests that this may also be in part due to the availability of cheap – generally female – labour, suitable for training in assembly work, there.

Certainly, the Massey-Meegan type of analysis should be extended to other kinds of industry. In particular, we need firmer empirical evidence on what happens to those rendered redundant by closures or reductions in output – in particular, on the extent of de-skilling. And we need also to understand whether the process will vary in local labour markets of different size and character.

Technological change[9]

The processes described need to be understood, in part, as a response to technological change. The economy, after all, does not exist within an inert atmosphere. The life cycles of different cities have been associated with technological changes, which in turn are influenced by the development of manufacturing, management, and distributive techniques and even by innovative ideas in planning, coordination, and control. The urban firm both influences its technological environment

[9]This subsection was drawn from the literature review by Goddard and Thwaites (1980) *The Inner City in Context*, Paper 4.

and is influenced by it. Technological changes, by creating new industries, destroying others, and changing the optimal locations of activities, can make the fortunes of regions and cities for good or ill. Some, by creating a need for new equipment, may stimulate investment and employment; others may have the reverse effect. Some may stimulate a demand for new skills; others may cause a substitution from high-skill (often male) jobs to unskilled female ones. Some may lead to less demand for space, others to more — with profound locational impacts (Goddard and Thwaites 1980, 7–10).

All this will vary greatly from industry to city depending on the local industrial mix. In some industries such as public utilities, transport and distribution, technological change has already dramatically reduced employment and future job prospects, with serious effects on inner city economies. In others, the impact is probably still to come. One fact of great potential importance is that until now, investment per employee in office jobs has been much less than in production jobs — yet it is in the office sector that new technology, based on the microprocessor, may have its greatest effect in the 1980s; we speculate on this question in Chapter 6. Since cities are the location of so many of these jobs, the impact on employment could be particularly severe.

R and D — and the small firm

Many observers have suggested that the small firm may provide an important approach to economic rejuvenation in depressed areas such as inner cities. But the fact is that, from the limited available evidence, such small firms seem to attempt relatively little R and D and so are unlikely to be at the forefront of innovative technological development. Indeed, related to the earlier argument about take-overs, it may be that there are thresholds to R and D which may exclude the small firm altogether.

The main reason for this seems to be that as technology has become more specific and more complex, and as division of labour has taken place, the search for technological knowledge has become increasingly professionalised, with large numbers of specialists employed to carry out research tasks. Therefore, if a firm is to advance technologically, it needs not only to take part in research and to maintain contact with other research, but also to recruit its own scientific personnel — which small firms in inner city locations conspicuously cannot do. Thus detached R and D laboratories are principally found in the South East outside London, where private and public laboratories may enjoy external economies of contact and easy recruitment of qualified labour.

Small enterprises are relatively more innovative in this area than elsewhere in the country. R and D plants seem particularly prone to be split from the manufacturing function and to relocate on green-field sites outside the city. The presence in the city of large, often technologically oriented universities and polytechnics does not offer a countervailing force, since — contrary to American experience — British universities do not seem to function as major sources of industrial innovation. Thus the inner city is not likely to benefit from new manufacturing industry of an innovatory kind. Again, it is the smaller cities of the South East which are likely to be the main beneficiaries (Goddard and Thwaites 1980, Chapter 9).

This may seem odd. Traditionally, the inner city has been seen as an area favourable to the birth and development of innovative manufacturing firms. The well-known industrial quarters of Birmingham and East London, based on the external economies that small firms could obtain in close proximity, are often quoted as examples. But it seems that this advantage may have disappeared in the face of increasingly sophisticated technology and the need for professional R and D, coupled with the possibility that innovating individuals of the new kind may have migrated to suburbs or small towns. There is some evidence that in a given industry — electronics — inner London firms are less productive, probably because the more enterprising firms migrate out, leaving the older and less innovative companies behind (McDermott 1978, 541—50).

Yet the very limited work so far suggests that the inner city can still provide a favourable location for small new firms, because of factors like capital availability, personal contact and the existence of redundant plants. If this is true even in some measure — and in London the evidence is that small firms find capital hard to get — then as a matter of policy it seems essential that local authorities ensure an adequate supply of suitable premises for such firms. Large-scale redevelopment, it is argued, has perversely worked in the opposite direction, by drastically reducing the supply of older, low-rent properties on which small new firms depend. Here, as elsewhere, there is little empirical evidence — though one study suggests that many firms may find redevelopment a positive advantage, so long as they get financial compensation which they can then use as an assisted passage to better accommodation and higher productivity (Chalkley 1979, 12—13). Premises are almost certainly not the only limiting factor, however. Small firms may be inhibited by the rationalisation of purchasing and subcontracting, especially by central government and its agencies, who may be unwilling to take risks with new or small firms. Similarly, small firms may find it difficult to raise capital either from the banks, or from central local authorities.

Qualified pessimism

The only reasonable conclusion about the employment prospects of the inner city, then, must be one of qualified pessimism. The prospects are certainly not good but neither are they entirely hopeless. They probably vary a great deal from city to city. First, it seems clear that locational preferences for a wide range of economic activities have changed profoundly. Cities, and in particular inner cities, used to offer special advantages of linkages, good communications — including face-to-face contact — and other external economies to a wide range of manufacturing and service industries. Now, advances in transportation and communications — the national motorway network connecting almost every major city, high-speed trains, the network of telecommunications — have spread these advantages to very many other locations. At the same time, physical obsolescence and social malaise make the inner city a less attractive place both for employers and their key employees. They exercise their right to choose the places they like to live in and work in, and — increasingly — these places are anywhere but in the inner city. Even in the case of London, arguably the most resilient of Britain's inner city economies, it has become possible to assert that 'Without the advantages bequeathed to us from our history, the metropolis would have collapsed long ago' (Eversley, forthcoming).

Secondly, this effect is exacerbated by the notorious structural crisis of British industry — itself a reaction, in part, to the fact of vigorous competition from other highly-productive and well-equipped industrial countries — which finds its most extreme manifestation in the inner city. 'The processes of merger, rationalisation and re-equipment which seek to promote the necessary rises in national productivity and profitability may well have quite drastic negative effects on the availability of blue-collar jobs in the inner-urban areas' (Dicken and Lloyd 1979, 61). The main levers of change lie with the larger firms, and they are likely to continue being thrown in a way detrimental to the inner city.

Thirdly, therefore, the main hope for employment generation must lie with the small firm and its innovative capacities. But, as we have seen, these are very much in doubt. The process of growth in any case may be slow, and gains built up painfully over a long period may be wiped out with the death or movement of a firm or a plant. The balance of the evidence is that small inner city firms are neither very innovative nor very dynamic in terms of production or employment. To base a major strategy on them, in present circumstances, would seem highly dubious.

That is the pessimistic view. It may be modified by the current trend toward miniaturisation of many advanced techniques, which may make them more freely available to small firms, giving them greater competitive advantage (or, more accurately, less disadvantage) compared with the established bigger firms. Additionally, it appears that some cities — London, Birmingham, Manchester — have a higher proportion of dynamic small firms than others. In such cities, 'Policy should indeed be devised and applied which will nurture this particular segment of the city's economic base' (Dicken and Lloyd 1979, 60-1). But the prospects for other cities lacking this seedbed function — the Liverpools and Glasgows — may well be poor. Dicken and Lloyd's own balanced conclusion, based on their experience in the North West, is pessimistic:

> . . . the prospects for an industrial revival of the inner areas cannot be regarded as other than bleak. (Dicken and Lloyd 1979, 61).

Closing the Circle — Unemployment and Labour Markets

At the start of this chapter, we stressed the interrelatedness of its parts. As the chapter draws to its end, we logically seek to close the circle. Labour demand and supply are related in a complex chain of cause and effect with demographic changes, with migration, and with structural economic change that causes employment gains in some areas and employment losses in others. The residual item that closes this circle is unemployment — and, closely associated with it, variations in labour force participation, especially women.

Unemployment has long been used as a critical indicator of the health of local labour markets, of social inequality and of demographic experience. Despite substantial efforts over several decades to diminish the uneven distribution of job opportunities, there is some evidence that the local variations in employment rates, as well as the national average rate, are again on the increase.

Regional and other variations

Unemployment rates (excluding school leavers) in Great Britain have ranged between 1 percent in the mid-1950s to 6.4 percent in mid-1980. Consistently, higher-than-average rates have been reported for Northern Ireland, Scotland, the North and Wales; lower-than-average rates for the South East, East Anglia, and the Midlands. Less well reported are the even wider variations within regions. Metropolitan Counties, together with Central Clydeside, had nearly 40 percent of total British unemployment in 1976; Greater London alone had nearly 12 percent of the total. Throughout the 1970s, inner city unemployment has been about twice as high as in outer areas, and towards the end of the decade the differential was growing. Inner London tends to have as many unemployed workers in absolute terms as the whole of Scotland, and, despite having lost over 100,000 economically active males in seven years, its total of unemployed has doubled. Nevertheless, it should be stressed that not all Metropolitan Counties have higher than average unemployment rates: in 1976 Merseyside, Tyneside, and South East Lancashire (Greater Manchester) and Clydeside were above the average, the rest below it.

Small pockets of very bad unemployment tend to exist within the inner areas of conurbations. The paradox is that these often seem to occur within reasonable travelling distance of other areas with relatively low rates of unemployment. Part of the explanation may lie with the uncharted operations of the 'informal economy', which may provide additional income to the registered unemployed — and on which a great deal of research demands to be done. As with the study of employment trends, we need to understand in more detail who becomes unemployed, and to ascertain whether different unemployment profiles exist between different areas.

Unemployment profile

As to the question of who is unemployed, there is one important generalisation: the incidence of unemployment among the unskilled is higher than for other groups wherever they may live (Thrift 1979, 169-72). In some inner cities — particularly London — the paradox now exists of high rates of unemployment and of vacant jobs side-by-side: the jobs are skilled ones needing education and training, which the unemployed conspicuously lack. Therefore, education, training, and retraining are likely to form an important part of the solution to the problem. The 1971 data showed that for any given socioeconomic group, there seemed to be no general tendency for unemployment rates to be higher in inner than in outer boroughs; the main reason why inner areas may have higher unemployment is that they contain more unskilled people.

Age is also a factor, in that the young and the old tend towards unemployment to a greater extent than the middle-aged groups. In particular, the baby boom of 1955-65 manifested itself during the 1970s in relatively large numbers of school-leavers coming onto the labour market at a time of recession, and this effect was particularly dire in the traditional high-fertility areas (Belfast, Clydeside, Merseyside) where many of these school-leavers also happened to lack skills. Even so, age by itself is not as important as skill (Thrift 1979, 172). In any event, the 'bulge' of young school leavers will again begin to turn down after 1981.

The ethnic factor is undoubtedly of significance. After standardising for qualifications, unemployment is significantly higher among the West Indian population, though there is some evidence that blacks were more likely to visit the school careers officer and to be persistent in job applications than were whites (Commission for Racial Equality 1978, 8). It is true that a majority of both groups are in work and a majority of the unemployed are neither young nor black; but this reflects the obvious fact that a majority of the population are neither young nor black. Certainly, the proportion of blacks — especially young blacks — who are unemployed is very much higher than for whites, and the absolute differences may be growing (Smith 1977, 71; CRE 1978, 10).

Recruitment and job search

There is in fact a whole series of unanswered questions about the operation of the labour market, especially concerning recruitment and job search. They include the locational characteristics and variations of the ways in which firms recruit workers, and the ways in which young workers search for and obtain jobs; the varying role of accessibility and the journey to work, especially for young workers; the effect of union closed shops and apprenticeship schemes; and the likely patterns of new recruitment by different industries, given the present age composition of the workforce. There is a role, here, for studies that distinguish the inner city as an area of distinctively different labour market relationships, as against the rest of the space economy. But at the same time, we should not exaggerate the differences: it remains true, for areas as for groups of people, that a majority of inner city workers are not unemployed and that a majority of all unemployment is outside inner city areas however they are conventionally defined.

Such research into processes can help avoid the obvious pitfalls of purely statistical analysis. To say that unskilled people are more prone to become unemployed may be useful as a starting point, but it does not tell us how and why they became unemployed (or if they were previously unemployed). It is similar with the phenomenon of labour force participation rates, especially for women. Population growth in the rings, and the fact that women tend to work close to their homes, have tended to cause high participation rates there and in other areas where surplus female labour is available. It has been suggested that firms have actually moved into areas with such surpluses, so as to be able to exploit their relative cheapness and lack of organisation (Massey 1976, 9). Rising participation rates in such areas – ranging from metropolitan rings in the south to older industrial areas, with no previous tradition of female work, in the north – may thus be the counterpart of skilled male unemployment in the urban cores.

Labour supply and demand

The final crucial question concerns the relationship of demand for labour and supply of labour, and the mismatch between the two. For any given level of unemployment in 1980, there are more vacancies than five years before. 'We are afflicted by a wasteful mismatch of workers and jobs. And it is getting worse' (Palmer and Gleave 1978, 454). The supply of labour will depend on job turnover (entries and exits), occupational mobility, job enrichment actually on the job, and labour migration. It has been suggested that there is a relationship between occupational and geographical mobility. Though it is true that higher-skill groups tend to be willing and able to move farther to change jobs, the relationships is by no means simple or clear.

Geographical mobility

What is perhaps clearer are the barriers to geographical mobility. Housing policy in Britain – with its progressively diminishing private rental sector, its highly immobile public rental sector, and its relatively high transaction costs for owner-occupiers who move – has undoubtedly acted as a serious brake on mobility, especially of the longer-distance kind that may be necessary to effect a change in employment. Government attitudes toward assisting labour migration have been mixed and even contradictory. Nevertheless, the Employment Transfer Scheme did help some 25,000 workers (and their families) to move during 1976/7 alone. A partial assessment of the scheme has been made (Beaumont in McLennan and Parr 1979, 65-80), but more work is needed. As against this, the 'key workers' scheme, whereby preferential treatment is given to skilled workers – for instance, in moving to new towns – tends to discriminate against the less skilled, or those who are under-represented there. One ironic result is that the Industrial Selection Scheme for the new towns has been taking skilled workers out of the conurbations, while the employment transfer scheme brought them in. Similarly, the key workers scheme brought skilled workers into the Development Areas, while the Employment Transfer Scheme took them out (Johnson and Salt 1978, 13).

An obvious alternative to migration for work is to extend the local search for work by extending the daily commuting trip. But, as we earlier noticed, the rise in car ownership may perversely reduce the potential mobility of those who remain dependent on public transport. The conurbations are characterised by lower car ownership levels than in the country as a whole; public transport patronage is correspondingly higher. Yet the public transport system, as elsewhere, is caught in a vicious circle of rising costs and falling fare incomes. By the early 1980s there were ominous signs that a number of British conurbation public transport systems, including London, the West Midlands and Greater Manchester, were unable to continue to operate without massive subsidy that was unlikely to be forthcoming.

Yet the great majority of lower paid unskilled and semi-skilled workers depend for access to work either on the bus or on walking or cycling, all of which modes are slow and so do not offer a very large potential commuter field. Thus, despite increasingly rapid decentralisation of jobs, there is no commensurate increase in reverse commuting. Only in London does the rail system offer much potential for this — and even there the cost might well be prohibitive. In a conurbation like Liverpool, as the Inner Area Study pointed out, the city boundaries form the effective outer commuter limits for inner city residents.

However, it is not immediately clear whether transport improvements would substantially benefit the accessibility of inner area residents to jobs. Gillespie (1980, 52—62) follows Bentham (1978, 158—60) in arguing that it would, but insofar as there is a city-wide or conurbation-wide deficiency of demand for unskilled workers, this would not be true. Thus McGregor (1980) finds that for Glasgow the main cause of unemployment is not the 'mismatch' between jobs and job-seekers in different parts of the city, whereas for London mismatch almost certainly does provide part of the explanation. The critical question is whether low-skill jobs are available outside the inner area and within potential commuting distance. Certainly, it appears that in view of the concentration of low-skill workers in the inner cities any one strategy on its own is unlikely to achieve much success. Even if better accessibility to jobs outside the inner areas will help, it will need to be accompanied by assistance to migration, by training schemes, and if possible by the creation of new unskilled jobs within the inner areas themselves.

Several times in this discussion, we have remarked upon the critical importance of industrial restructuring. Given that fact, it seems important to know just how far this process is associated with labour movement. Most moves by private company workers are of a normal kind, made between different locations of a multi-plant company, particularly among higher-level managerial and professional workers. More significant for our purpose are the moves made as a result of plant closure or plant transfer — and about this, as about other moves within companies, little is known (Johnson and Salt 1978, 15). But almost certainly, the bulk of manual workers are recruited at the new site.

Occupational mobility

The obvious alternative to direct geographical mobility is occupational mobility — which may allow a displaced worker to find another job in the same area, or may render him better equipped to move. At the beginning of the 1980s, industrial retraining schemes are of negligible importance, with a mere 22,000 places available in 'Skillcentres' in 1980–1. With the great increase in the number of unemployed unskilled workers in the cities, coupled with the paradoxical existence of vacancies in other industrial sectors within the urban economy, it is not surprising that there is again much interest in retraining. Yet in London, for instance, the Skillcentres are poorly located to meet the needs of the disadvantaged, mainly because of their need for space and access to an 'engineering environment' (Leonard 1979, 3), though in other smaller cities, however, the Skillcentres are probably within reasonable travel distance (Reid 1976, 16). Larger barriers may exist in the perceptions and the knowledge of the people who need to be reached. Furthermore — a little researched or understood field — the retrained worker may then find further obstacles in finding a job, because employers in conjunction with trades unions protect their existing workforce by insisting on formal apprenticeship qualifications.

Summary

Profound changes are taking place in the industrial structure of contemporary Britain. They are associated with large and relatively rapid relative shifts in the location of economic activities. These tend to take the form of closure and contraction in certain places coupled with expansion in others, rather than of actual relocation. Industrial acquisition is a strong contributory factor. The main impact is large-scale closure of older (but not necessarily less innovative or productive) plants in the inner cities, with big losses of employment (chiefly male, and often skilled), accompanied by only modest gains in employment (often unskilled and female) in the new locations. In the process, few of the displaced workers move.

From then on, the prospects of these workers are fairly dire. The remaining indigenous economy, though it varies in resilience from city to city, often tends to be dominated by older, less innovative and less competitive firms or plants. The seedbed or innovative function indeed appears largely to have deserted the inner cities for the smaller or medium-sized towns of southern England. Even office activity is under-represented in the cities outside London, and is dominated by more routine functions employing semi-skilled females, and much of it is highly prone to be replaced by new technology in the 1980s. Further, both the geographical and occupational mobility of labour are low because of a combination of unfortunate factors that include inflexible housing policies (especially in the public rented sector where so many manual workers are now housed) and lack of large-scale retraining schemes. In addition, the massive evidence of physical obsolescence of the physical plant is reinforced by the perception that governments are unwilliing or unable to spend much money on renewing it. All these facts, in evidence even before the mid-1970s, have since then been exacerbated by the world recession that has exposed the inner cities as a kind of soft underbelly of the British economy. Thus the problems of the inner cities form an extreme version of the woes of the British economy in general. Though there are some patches of light and the picture is by no means one of unrelieved gloom, no one should suppose that the future of the inner cities and their people is very bright.

Some Unanswered Questions

At the end of this long review of the state of the art, a whole series of unanswered questions remain and are open for further research. We summarise them briefly here, and return to them in the research agenda which forms the final chapter of this book.

The first concerns the relationship between structural change, at the national and the international scale, and the local economy. We know that the British economy in general Has been performing relatively poorly in competition with its international rivals, that its industries have been under-capitalised, that some of its sectors — especially in manufacturing, less so in advanced services — have shown particular weaknesses which may even be spreading, and that in these weak areas some firms may be particularly prone to take-over by more powerful and aggressive firms. From this it follows that we need more work on the processes that operate within the economy at different spatial scales. We need particularly to look at the attitudes of large corporations to the inner city; at the so-called seedbed function that the inner city has traditionally performed for small firms, but that many believe is now disappearing; and at the entrepreneurial milieu that the inner city represents for economic innovation, in competition with other locations. Particularly, here, we should look not merely at the locations that seem to be failing, but also — indeed even more intensely — at those that seem to be succeeding, to see what if anything can be learned from them.

Secondly, we should be looking at the impact of structural changes upon local labour markets. One of the most disturbing features of inner city economies is the phenomenon of mismatch, whereby unemployment and unfilled job vacancies can exist side-by-side. We should study how these might be brought into some kind of better relationship — and, in particular, whether the constraints are primarily those of education and skill, or of time and distance that separate jobs from people. But we may need to relate this topic to a third: that of the informal economy, which may represent an important — albeit un-recorded — element in the whole economic structure of the inner city. The focus should be particularly on the subtle and shifting boundary line that separates the formal from the informal economy for different groups of the urban population, and on the ways in which individuals move from one economy to the other. This, we feel, could powerfully illuminate some of the paradoxes that seem to exist in the economic life of the contemporary inner city.

3   Deprivation in the Inner City

Peter Hall and Susan Laurence

The long discussion in Chapter 2 of economic and social change leads logically to a critical question: why worry? If people are leaving the inner city for homes and jobs in the suburbs and exurbs, if inner urban industries are closing down faster than others open up and office jobs are not taking their place in sufficient numbers, why should we be concerned? After all, Britain since World War Two has been a market economy modified by planning. The political-philosophical consensus, shared of course not by all but certainly by most, has been that people should have the freedom to take critical decisions that affect their own lives — such as moving home or job, starting or closing a business — so long as by so doing they do not inflict serious side effects on others. Politicians and planners have not seen it as their job (though occasionally they have behaved as if they did) to freeze the pattern of social and economic development as it happened to exist at one point in time. Cities, demonstrably, are loosening up and opening out; in Brian Berry's words, 'the glue of concentration has dissolved' (Berry, forthcoming). Surely, unless the effects are seriously negative, they should be allowed to do so.

But there is a strong, complicating argument. Inner cities, some people have suggested, represent a serious problem for public policy because they contain exceptionally large concentrations of poor and disadvantaged people. Not only is this serious in itself; the degree of concentration, it is argued, helps to ensure that the process is cumulative, in that poverty and deprivation are transmitted from generation to generation, through poor nurture and poor education in the formative years. This has been a powerful theme running through the academic literature on the subject in the past two decades, first in discussing the problems of Third World cities, later in extension to the cities of the developed world. In the words of its leading exponent, Oscar Lewis, the 'culture of poverty' is 'a way of life, remarkably stable and persistent, passed on from generation to generation along family lines' (Lewis

1961, xxiv). But it has also inspired political action. The Community Action Programs in the United States in the mid-1960s, the Educational Priority Areas and the Urban Programme in Britain from the late 1960s, all reflected the notion that compensatory spending ought to be concentrated on deprived areas. And in a celebrated speech of 1972 Sir Keith Joseph deliberately espoused the Lewis thesis when he developed the idea of transmitted deprivation, which — he claimed — persisted despite generally improving standards of living in the society at large (Joseph 1972, 1—10).

Ever since its original formulation the idea has been critically attacked. Indeed Sir Keith Joseph has publicly accepted that SSRC-conducted research has disproved the whole concept by showing that, 'As many people escape from the way of life of unloving and unskilful parents as are imprisoned by it' (Joseph 1979, 7). One widespread view is that there is indeed a special kind of sub-culture of poverty, which people use to make sense of the situation in which they find themselves at that particular time (Gans 1971, 146—64). Ken Pryce has vividly described such a sub-culture among young men of West Indian descent in St Paul's, the inner urban area of Bristol that later became the scene of riots (Pryce 1979, 727—30). Yet, for politicians and policy-makers the idea of transmitted deprivation seems to exert a morbid fascination: they worry about it, perhaps, because they realise that if there were any truth in it, their efforts at social improvement could never be ultimately successful. For this reason, and for the reason that concentrations of poverty and deprivation are significant in their own right, there has been continuing academic interest in such concentrations — and, associatedly, the debate on poverty, both in the United States and Britain, has focused on the question of geographical concentrations of deprivation, and of the wisdom of the area priority approach. This chapter tries to synthesise that debate, so as to provide a better framework of critical understanding for the discussion of public policy approaches in Chapter 6. But first, as a necessary preliminary, we need to review some definitions of poverty and deprivation.

Poverty and Deprivation

Poverty, it might be thought, could be defined simply as lack of resources, or as lack of the income that buys access to resources. But there are difficult problems of what to include in income, and what not. Most official estimates are based on a concept of marketable wealth. But there are many forms of indirect income and non-marketable assets which do not figure in official statistics: pension rights, equity shares, gifts of wealth and property transfers, and tax evasion in the 'informal sector'. A better definition would include all these; Townsend's monumental study (Townsend 1979) tries to do so, supplementing official information by questionnaire surveys.

There are equally difficult problems involved in defining a level of poverty or deprivation. The current approach still owes much to nineteenth-century pioneers like Booth and Rowntree, who established the notion of the 'poverty line': an absolute minimum of existence, below which a household's income should not be allowed to fall. This is the basis of the official standard used to determine payment of Supplementary Benefit. But clearly, in a society above subsistence level, the notion of poverty is not an absolute one, but is related to some kind of social norm. Townsend, in a much-quoted definition, regards poverty as 'the lack of the resources necessary to permit participation in the activities, customs and diets commonly approved by society' (Townsend 1979, 88). From this he suggests a relative income standard that relates income distributions to a mean; and also a relative deprivation standard, which considers whether an individual or household has access to a number of goods and services that constitute a kind of national average style of living — such as holidays taken, visits made, visitors entertained, and meals taken — which prove to correlate closely with income.

Townsend finds that in 1968, the year of his survey, 7.1 percent of the households in Britain were 'in poverty' on the official definition, in that they had incomes below the Supplementary Benefit standard plus housing costs, but, in addition, 23.8 percent of households could be said to be on the margin of poverty, in that their incomes were less than 40 percent above that level. In terms of his alternative relative income standard, 10.6 percent were 'in poverty' in that their incomes were 50 per cent or more below the mean; another 29.5 per cent were on the margin, with incomes 20-50 per cent below the mean. Finally, in terms of Townsend's own relative deprivation standard, 25.2 per cent lacked the incomes associated with a standard pattern of consumption of goods and services (Townsend 1979, 273).

The critical question is what kinds of people and households fall below the poverty line. Townsend finds that 'the risks of being in poverty vary dramatically according to age, employment status, family type and, especially, occupational class' (1979, 898). The choice between his three standards did not make much difference. Elderly people who had been unskilled manual workers, especially those with a history of unemployment, sickness or disablement, or single parent families, were most likely to be poor. About one third of income units in poverty, according to the official standard, contained a disabled or long-time ill person; about one third contained a person of pensionable age; and of the remaining third — which contained a person in employment — about half belonged to the low-paid. The numbers are substantial: a total of 17.6 million people in all (Townsend 1979, 902).

Since Townsend's 1968 survey, some of these figures may have significantly changed. The proportions of the elderly have grown; so have the numbers of long-term unemployed; so, fairly spectacularly, have the numbers of one-person families. All this suggests that in quantitative terms the problem of poverty may not have got any better since 1968. The likelihood, indeed, is that it has got a good deal worse.

Areal Variations in Poverty and Deprivation

The crucial question for our study, though, is to what extent poverty and deprivation are concentrated significantly in certain areas — above all in the inner cities. On this point, there is now a considerable volume of work: Peter Townsend's study, the Royal Commission on the Distribution of Income and Wealth, studies by Webber, Holtermann and others. Broadly, they come to the same conclusion: that concentrations do exist, but that there are many poor people outside them, while many in these areas are not poor. In other words, geography is far from the most important factor in helping to understand the causes of deprivation.

Townsend's conclusion

Townsend's most important conclusion was that poverty is very widely dispersed: though there were variations from place to place, rich and poor were to be found everywhere. In the poorest group of districts distinguished in his analysis, one-quarter of the population was relatively prosperous, while in the richest group 14 percent had incomes below or only just above the poverty standard. Putting it another way, no less than 46 percent of the poor or marginally poor were found in two income areas (out of four in his analysis) with the highest average incomes.

There were however some small areas in some cities with greater concentrations of poverty: in part of Salford 38 percent were poor, in a part of Glasgow 48 percent, in a part of Belfast 50 percent. (The comparable figure for the entire United Kingdom was 28 percent.) These areas had high concentrations of one-parent families, of unemployed males, of manual workers and especially of unskilled manual workers. About half the exceptional degree of poverty in these areas could be explained by class structure. Also important were incomes, housing, large families and one-parent families (Townsend 1979, 553—60). However, Townsend has to conclude, overall, that

> . . . there are areas with about twice as many poor or marginally poor as in the nation as a whole. These areas also have a disproportionately high prevalence of other types of deprivation. But there are two major reservations: (a) the majority of poor are not to be found in areas which even account for 20 percent of the poor; and (b) there are substantial minorities of relatively prosperous people even in the poorest districts of the country. (1979, 548)

Overall, therefore, however we define deprived areas, it will be true that — unless we include nearly half the areas in the country, which makes the exercise meaningless — there will be more poor persons living outside them than within them. Further, within the deprived areas there will be more non-deprived people than deprived people. Therefore, Townsend concludes: 'Discrimination based on ecology will miss out more of the poor and deprived than it will include. It will also devote resources within the area to people (or children) who are not poor or deprived' (1979, 556).

Confirmation from other sources

The above conclusion is powerfully reinforced by a considerable volume of other work using either direct measurement of incomes or the social indicators approach. Thus the Royal Commission on Incomes and Wealth, while it acknowledged significant variations in the distribution of income, had reservations about the importance of the spatial dimension: 'regional differences in income by themselves do not stand out in comparison with other causes in the variation of income of households and families' (Royal Commission 1978, 43). Similarly, a number of studies using social indicators suggest that differences between one part of the country and another are not large, and that the differences between individuals and households within any one area are more important than the differences between the averages for one area and another (Hall 1980a, 331). True, many of these studies (McCallister, Parry and Rose 1979; Smith 1979) work at the relatively coarse areal level of the standard region, so that they do not say anything directly about the condition of the inner city. But it is perhaps significant that regions containing large cities with substantial older inner areas demonstrate poor social indicators in such matters as infantile mortality or staying on at school after 16. However, this does not hold universally: Northern Ireland, which consistently shows the lowest incomes and the worst social indicators, contains substantial rural areas as well as Belfast; while Greater London, at or near the top on many indicators, is certainly the most highly urbanised.

Income data at a more disaggregated level, by county, certainly reinforce the fact that 'Low income households live in both urban and rural areas' (Thomas and Winward in Shaw 1979, 21), although the western Celtic fringe of Cornwall, Devon, Powys and Gwynedd — rural and remote from the British industrial core — come right at the foot of the ladder (Shaw 1979, 22). Further, low pay is a much more serious problem in rural areas than in Britain generally: the New Earnings Survey shows clearly that, here, men are relatively poorly paid, in comparison to the national average, in the South West and in East Anglia, while women in those regions — who are nearer the national average — are nevertheless still below it (Shaw 1979, 26). The authors of this particular analysis conclude, with some justification, that the concern with inner city deprivation has arisen because the urban poor are more visible, and are seen as a threat to social order in a way that the rural poor are not (Shaw 1979).

Holtermann's analysis

At the relatively coarse grain of the region or county, therefore, there is powerful evidence — both from incomes and from social indicators — that poverty is far from being an exclusively or predominantly urban phenomenon; and that in any area, both rich and poor are found. That conclusion is confirmed at a finer grain by the work of other researchers such as Sally Holtermann and Richard Webber. Holtermann's analysis, based on 1971 Census data for enumeration districts — the smallest areas for which such data are available 87,000 of them in Great Britain — takes a variety of social indicators, and computes for each the distribution of the worst 5 percent of enumeration districts. Though differences emerge as between one area and another, they seldom demonstrate a consistent pattern. Thus the inner London boroughs show up badly on housing: with 8.6 percent of all EDs in Great Britain, they have nearly 22 percent of the worst areas from the point of view of overcrowding and lack of amenities. Yet on unemployment, they show up well with only 2.9 percent of the worst EDs. Conversely, Greater Manchester and Merseyside score well on overcrowding, but poorly on basic amenities or unemployment. The sole exception is Central Clydeside, the Glasgow conurbation: it consistently has more than its share of every form of social deprivation, having 4.3 percent of all EDs yet a staggering 37 percent of the worst EDs on overcrowding, over 13 percent on lack of amenities, and 23 percent for unemployed (Holtermann 1975, 40–1).

There is however an important gloss: some not particularly urbanised regions, such as central Scotland, also show a high concentration of the most deprived EDs. Further, Holtermann confirms other studies in showing that the great majority of deprived people were found outside the most deprived areas. The worst 5 percent of enumeration districts contained only 23 percent of all households lacking or sharing a hot water supply, only 15 percent of those suffering severe male unemployment, and only 18 percent of those lacking exclusive use of all basic amenities. Further, she found very little evidence of multiple deprivation at an ED level in that the worst districts on one criterion were almost invariably not the worst on another — though the conclusion can be criticised, in that she omitted many non-housing criteria, and her technique (of simple addition of criteria) was relatively simplistic.

More recent studies

Holtermann's 1975 work is powerfully confirmed by a series of more recent studies that also employ the social indicators approach. David Smith, looking at enumeration districts within London, finds an 'absence of a close coincidence between different criteria' of deprivation (Smith D.M. 1979, 205), and notes additional evidence in a Department of Health and Social Security study (Imber 1977, *passim*) and in the maps in the Social Atlas of London (Shepherd, Westaway and Lee 1974, *passim*). Hamnett reached a similar conclusion after quoting a study of the London boroughs of Newham and Southwark by Hatch and Shervott: 'areas suffering from multiple deprivation do not seem to form a quite separate category easily distinguished from other less deprived areas (Hamnett 1976, 11).

An official study by the Department of the Environment tried to cluster wards within conurbations, and other large urban areas, into consistent types, using different social indicators, but failed to distinguish a common set of areas — either in terms of social location or internal characteristics — that could be labelled the most deprived. Though the vast majority of wards in conurbations were suffering from above-average levels of deprivation on one or another indicator, there was little consistency in the pattern of variation (Department of the Environment 1975, *passim*).

Webber's vital contribution

The most important work in this genre, however, is undoubtedly that of Richard Webber, first applied to Merseyside (Webber 1975) and then generally across the country. It used principal components analysis to produce bundles of social indicators that went together in certain enumeration districts. One such bundle contained the classic signs of deprivation: high unemployment, lack of skilled jobs, poor educational achievement levels, high crime rates, and other indicators of social malaise. The enumeration districts that scored high rates were nearly all in the city of Liverpool itself, hardly at all in the outer parts of the city. And the very worst rates were in Exchange ward, a classic inner urban area close to the city centre. There is evidence here, then, of concentration. But Webber also found that there were emerging indices of serious deprivation in some of the outer council estates — above all in Speke (DoE 1977C, 95). Thus the deprived inner city, Webber's work suggests, is not so much a geographical state as a social state. Its home until now has been in the inner areas, because that is where historical circumstances have caused many people to become deprived. But it can be displaced outside the city altogether, by the planned movement of 'problem' individuals and families into what becomes a new problem milieu. In any event, many individuals will always escape the trap; even in the most deprived areas, a majority of individuals and households will not be deprived according to whatever index is being used.

Nevertheless it does remain true that some areas in cities show greater concentrations of overall deprivation than do others. To that extent, the argument for an area-based approach may be justified. And this receives further backing from the 1977 National Dwellings and Housing Survey, which gives evidence suggesting that since 1971 the problem may have accentuated, with an increasing degree of spatial concentration of deprivation.

We can sum up the conclusion so far: some areas put individuals and people at greater risk of becoming poor or deprived, but many will escape the trap. It is a matter of statistical probability, not of determinate certainty. That conclusion is notably reinforced by an important study of social indicators nation-wide, by Donnison and Soto (Donnison and Soto 1980). They work at the level of whole local authorities, and so do not capture fine differences between inner and outer areas. But they do cover comparatively the whole urban system according to whether individual cities and towns provide a good life for their inhabitants — and especially for their children, in terms of the life chances available through the educational system. They are especially concerned about the conditions and opportunities of the less advantaged: the manual workers, in particular the unskilled ones, and the old.

The Good and the Bad City

Donnison and Soto find that overwhelmingly, the best places to live are the growing ones that depend on service industry (of both the private and public variety) and on the newer forms of manufacturing. That is true for everyone, but it is especially true for manual workers in general and for the unskilled ones in particular. In such places they are more likely to have a job, own a car, have better housing, and see their children doing well in school. Other vulnerable groups — women workers and single parents — also seem to do better. Thus they conclude: 'The growing prosperous city, the city which is kindest to its more vulnerable citizens and the city which distributes its opportunities more equally than most can all be the same place. At urban scale at least, we do not have to choose between progress and equality' (Donnison and Soto 1980, 176).

Perhaps most significant are the prosperous working-class towns in what Donnison and Soto call Middle England. They are fourteen towns, based on engineering, mainly in the southern half of England. By middle-class standards they are probably not very desirable places to live in; they actually contain more than their share of the vulnerable groups, and they have fewer people with 'A' levels or equivalent. Yet they seem to provide rather well for their inhabitants, their economies demanding middle-range skills for which middle-range incomes are paid. These in turn are matched with middle-price housing, and with educational systems equipped (among other things) to give their children middle-level skills. Such towns may make it relatively easy for people to move a notch at a time up the ladder of qualifications and incomes — though Donnison and Soto cannot prove it. Other kinds of town, such as the newer industrial suburbs in the conurbations and the new towns, may share these characteristics. For the average manual worker, such places truly represent the Good City.

In contrast, there is a Bad City. It consists of the declining cities of the conurbations, plus the towns of central Scotland. Like the Good Cities, these Bad Cities also have concentrations of manual workers in general, unskilled and semi-skilled manual workers in particular. But because their basic industries are declining, everyone loses ground: the skilled men lose opportunities for better jobs and higher earnings, and in turn they displace unskilled men into unemployment. Overall, then such places have high rates of male unemployment. Women do better because they take new unskilled or semi-skilled jobs in service and other non-manual occupations — though these may not pay very well. This however is not the end of the problem of the Bad City: in comparison to the towns of Middle England, it also delivers a relatively bad education system, at least in terms of measurable attainments, to its children. This is not particularly noticeable for the children of professional or managerial parents; it is most noticeable for the children of the less skilled. Perhaps that is because the prevailing economic and social ambience does not give children much incentive to work at school; on this interpretation, 'A town's educational attainment and its social composition may be more the effects than the causes of economic growth and urban development' (Donnison and Soto 1980, 155).

The root problem here is decline of the economic base. It subtly depresses the hopes and expectations of both parents and children. And, in a period of national stagnation or even overall national economic decline, the problem is exacerbated. But, it must be stressed again, there is no absolute rule: some children in the Bad City do advance up the educational and skill ladders, some children in Middle England fail to do so. The appropriate image is that of a handicap race: some entrants have a handicap, others not, but many factors will affect the outcome.

More specialised studies of other policy areas support that view. Thus, in housing, deprivation seems to be a problem of ethnic, occupational and household characteristics, not a specifically locational problem; though there are concentrations in inner cities, it can also be found in smaller industrial and mining communities and even in rural areas (Murie and Forrest 1980, Chapter 4). In health care, the unequal distribution of resources is said to have had the effect of 'making access to medical skills a lottery, according to where you live' (Pahl 1978, 678-81). However, the larger differences seem to be inter-regional rather than intra-urban; thus London does much better than the West Midlands conurbation, for instance. Another study does suggest that in general the conurbations had rather heavy health care needs, which in some cases were not being satisfied (Department of the Environment 1975, I, 26). At the very local scale, work in Newcastle upon Tyne shows that the distribution of tooth decay among schoolchildren is closely related to their access to dental services; but in fact parts of the inner city did better in this regard than did peripheral areas (Bradley, Kirby and Taylor 1978, 538).

Summing up

The evidence can be summed up thus. First, there are undoubted variations in poverty and deprivation between one area and another; there are real concentrations of deprivation, including different types of deprivation. But secondly, these patterns are by no means simple: the distribution of one kind of deprivation may be very different from that of another, and there is generally — save in one or two exceptional areas — no great degree of coincidence. Thirdly, concentrations of deprivation do tend to occur in inner urban areas, but they are by no means the only examples.

There is a curious policy conclusion, which may at first sight appear self-contradictory. Attempts to counter deprivation through area-based policies will on the one hand, tend to miss their target, in that they will help some people who do not need much help, and on the other fail to deliver help to some people who do need it. But there is nevertheless a case for area-based policies — not as a substitute for national policies that concentrate aid on the most needy families, but as a complement to them. Such policies would embrace those actions that are most conveniently taken on a local area basis: new or rehabilitated housing, new schools, better transport and shopping and community facilities.

The justification for such an approach is threefold. First, it probably represents an effective way of spending scarce resources without spreading them thinly and without recourse to means-testing or cumbrous eligibility rules (Holtermann 1978, 39). Secondly, it provides a learning experience for people administering local projects and even for those benefiting from them, which can be used progressively to improve the level of competence in subsequent local projects. Thirdly, and relatedly, it can have a demonstration effect both for the neighbourhood in question, where it may transform the local psychological climate from one of apathy and despair to one of hope and determination, and more widely for other similar communities which will be able to judge the resultant potential for change.

However, these policies should consist less in an attempt to disburse welfare to meet the consequences of decline, than in an attempt to grapple with its causes. The argument is that the forces of decline and decay are powerful and cumulative. As a local economy decays, redundant workers either migrate out of the area or become unemployed, leaving a population dominated by the elderly, the middle-aged and the poor. There is also a general feeling of physical decay both in private and in public housing, since the area becomes identified as a bad place to live in (Townsend 1979, 562).

All this will be immeasurably more difficult in the early 1980s than it would have been a decade previously. For local deprivation is no longer the residual problem that once it appeared to be. In an era of general economic decline many areas require special help. The problem is how to discriminate in favour of those among them that are hardest hit of all. The key is to try to identify those areas that had both a high concentration of economic and social deprivation during the 1970s, and also a heavy out-movement of people and jobs during the same period. And when this is done, the areas needing help will be seen to be not merely small pockets in inner urban areas, but rather whole metro-politan economies the size of Merseyside or Strathclyde. It is a daunting problem.

In such circumstances, vigorous action may be needed to attract both public and private capital back into the area, and so try to reverse the downward trend. But in order to achieve that, either at local or at national level, it will be necessary to understand the different forces at work. Industrial change, labour market and housing market behaviour, social service policies all interact to produce what we see in the inner city, and analysis of their interaction is a first step to policy formula-tion. As Peter Willmott stresses, this was indeed the approach of the inner city consultants' studies published in 1977, which marked a new approach to the problem in recognising the need for a combination of national policies and area-based approaches in places where dis-advantaged people were concentrated (Willmott 1980, 3). In Chapter 6, when we discuss policies, we shall see just how big a break this was. It marked a shift from treating consequences, toward tackling causes. Before however we turn to that history, we need to take a sideways look at the inner city worldwide and in particular at the American ex-perience — since this provided such an important original impetus to the whole British policy response.

4   The Inner City Worldwide

Peter Hall

This is the first of two chapters that form a diversion from the main theme — but, we believe, an important and useful one. In them, we open up the context to look at the position of the inner city outside Britain. First, in this chapter we attempt a summary review of the changes that are affecting cities and their surrounding regions in the major industrialised nations of the world. Secondly, in the chapter that follows we take a closer look at the United States — the country that proves to parallel Britain most closely in its recent patterns of urban change.

An Anglo-American Problem?

A useful starting-point for out study is to ask how far the inner city problem is a uniquely British — or, more accurately, an Anglo-American — problem. American urbanists were worrying about the decline of their cities even before the British became worried about theirs, and — to judge by some of the evidence presented below and in Chapter 5 — those worries were fully justified. But from the rest of the advanced industrial world — let alone the developing world where, notoriously, cities are growing at an unprecedented rate — the evidence seems more muted. Is it that the British and the Americans, both of them nations that industrialised early, have arrived first at some point on a continuum of change, to which other nations will inevitably arrive later? Or are there special features of their evolution that make their experience a bad guide for the rest of the world?

For the United States, a wealth of recent research evidence seems to agree that four basic trends are operating in the urban system. First, growth is tending to diffuse *downwards* through the urban hierarchy, from larger to smaller systems: larger metropolitan areas tend to be stagnating or even declining, smaller ones are still growing. Secondly, and in continuation of a process evident at least since the 1950s, growth is diffusing *outwards* through decentralisation within metropolitan areas, from cores to rings: cores (central cities) are often in rapid decline, while in most metropolitan areas (save one or two of the largest) surburban rings still continue to grow. Thirdly, and more recently, since 1970 the process of decentralisation has acquired a new dimension: growth is diffusing *further outwards* in a process of veritable de-urbanisation. The growth of metropolitan areas has sharply slowed down, while the non-metropolitan areas are now showing more rapid growth than the metropolitan ones. However, there is continuing controversy about the nature of this process. Much of the non-metropolitan growth is clearly occurring in contiguous counties just beyond the metropolitan limits, and so may be regarded as a further stage in the core-ring process, but a significant proportion is occurring in distant rural counties far outside metropolitan influence, where it appears to be related to development of natural resources, to tourism and to retirement (McCarthy and Morrison 1977, 1979; Vining and Straus 1977; Vining and Kontuly 1978; Vining in Kawashima 1981). Lastly and relatedly, growth is diffusing regionally, *away from* the older-industrialised and older-urbanised regions dominated by heavy industry (the North East, the Mid West) and *toward* the newly-industrialising and newly-urbanising regions, dominated by the newer high-technology industries and by services (the South, the West). Some of this growth, at least, is passing into non-metropolitan areas, but in the fast-growing regions the metropolitan areas also are demonstrating considerable dynamism.

These trends are discussed in greater detail in Chapter 5. Whatever the controversy within the research community as to the precise details, it is clear that the overwhelming trend is toward *deconcentration*: away from cities to suburbs, away from metropolitan areas to non-metropolitan ones, away from bigger agglomerations to smaller cities, and away from older-settled regions to newer, still more open ones. One observer (Berry 1976, Chapter 1) has gone so far as to label it a process of *counter-urbanisation*, in that it seems to represent a reversal of the well-established migration trends of the previous 200 years. Others doubt that, pointing out that some of the basic features — the more rapid growth of the South and West, the movement out of the cities, the stagnation of the largest urban areas — were already remarked upon in the 1930s (US National Resources Planning Board 1937, 285). Whatever the degree of continuity or disjuncture, it seems clear that American people — and American jobs — are deserting the older, larger central cities in the older industrial regions.

Britain, as Chapter 2 has shown in detail, is following many of the same trends. Population and employment are deserting urban cores for suburban rings and exurban outer rings; and these latter rings are equivalent to the contiguous non-metropolitan counties of the American analyses. The process happened earliest, and is now most advanced, in the largest metropolitan areas which are now losing people and jobs overall. The beneficiaries are smaller metropolitan areas some short distance away, as in the almost continuous ring 20—40 miles from London. At the same time there is a strong regional effect, with general metropolitan growth (save for London) throughout southern England, but general metropolitan stagnation or decline in much of northern England and Scotland. As with the American experience, these trends tend to merge. The general tendency is toward *deconcentration* from cities to suburbs, away from larger conurbation metropolitan areas toward smaller free standing ones, and away from the north and toward the south, so that the main result is a decline of the older, northern conurbations and a growth of the smaller, free standing urban systems of the southern half of England, in what are often quite rural areas. One result of these combined processes is that those left in the declining inner city areas find themselves progressively farther removed from the new job opportunities, so that one possible solution to their problems, reverse commuting out to the suburbs, becomes progressively less feasible.

European Trends

In continental Europe, at least until recently, the trends seem to have been very different. Recent work (Hall and Hay 1980) uses a metropolitan area framework of analysis — though the areas are drawn widely, to include what in American work would be termed contiguous non-metropolitan areas. It suggests that down to 1970, Europe presented a varied, and even confusing picture, in which different nations and regional blocks behaved in very different ways. And, insofar as any generalisation is possible, some of the trends seem to have been almost the reverse of the American ones.

Thus the great majority of Europeans live within metropolitan areas as defined in the study — and the proportion actually increased over the quarter century from 1950 to 1975. The non-metropolitan areas actually had fewer people in the mid-1970s than they had at the start of the 1950s. However, after 1960 there was a marked and increasing tendency toward decentralisation within metropolitan areas: the rings had a majority of the growth in the 1960s, and the whole of the growth in the early 1970s, as the growth in the cores suddenly ceased (Hall and

Hay 1980, 85–7). This evidence relates to Western Europe (and excludes some countries after 1970, for lack of data). For the two Eastern European countries that have been similarly studied, Poland and Hungary, no such trend toward decentralisation is observable (Hall 1980b, 49).

However, these overall trends conceal important differences between one regional part of Europe and another (Hall and Hay 1980, 89–153). *Atlantic Europe* (Great Britain and Ireland) demonstrated strong tendencies to decentralisation on the American model. But *Northern Europe* (Norway, Sweden, Denmark) again showed progressive decentralisation from cores to rings after 1960, with core populations falling after 1970; metropolitan areas grew somewhat, but much more weakly than non-metropolitan ones. *Western Europe* (Benelux, France), the most heterogenous subdivision, again showed a general tendency to decentralisation after 1960, with the rings' share of metropolitan growth rising from only 33 percent in the 1950s to no less than 69 percent in the 1970s. However, France proved a notable exception, with many metropolitan areas still centralising; it was anomalous, too, in being the only country where in the 1970s the non-metropolitan areas showed rapid growth.

In *Southern Europe* (Spain, Portugal, Italy) there was a rapid growth in metropolitan areas over the quarter century up to 1975, as peasant populations flooded in from the land. And, for most of this period, this flow was passing mainly into central cities, causing an actual tendency to centralisation – even in the largest metropolitan areas. But even here, decentralisation set in after 1970, with the rings growing twice as fast as the cores. *Central Europe* (the Federal Republic of Germany, Switzerland, Austria) began to decentralise earlier, from the 1960s. Unfortunately, data were almost entirely lacking after 1970 for the metropolitan area units used in the Hall/Hay study. Finally, the two countries that were studied in *Eastern Europe* (Hungary, Poland) showed sharp centralisation, with rapid growth of core cities and weaker growth (or even decline) of suburban rings; and this process actually intensified after 1970, as the declines in the ring areas accelerated.

The European Model

The European trends, then, are somewhat confusing. But we can fit them into a fairly consistent general model – at least if the two Eastern European countries are excluded. Generally, metropolitan areas grew rapidly while non-metropolitan areas lost – a product of a great migration of people, off the land and into the cities. (This process had no parallel in Great Britain or in the United States, for in both these countries it had been completed decades earlier.) In the 1950s, this led to a rapid growth of central city populations — and, where we have the data, of jobs. But after 1960 in Northern, Western and Central Europe, and after 1970 in Southern Europe, there was a general tendency to core-ring decentralisation. Eastern Europe has so far failed to demonstrate this transition — and this may reflect not merely differences in socio-political systems and related urban policies, but also the fact that these countries are at a still earlier state in industrial-urban evolution even than Southern Europe. We can, in other words, conceive of a trend toward decentralisation — a trend that affected the United States and Britain earliest and most fundamentally, then Northern, Western and Central Europe (with France providing something of an anomaly), then Southern Europe, and — perhaps, at some time in the future — will also affect Eastern Europe.

Overall, therefore, continental Europe appears to be at a somewhat earlier stage of evolution than either the United States or Britain. And this is supported by further evidence: that, unlike the United States, growth until recently has still been occurring in Europe's industrial heartland. During the period 1950-75 there was strong growth in the English Midlands, the area north and west of London, the eastern side of Randstad (Ring City) Holland, the Cologne-Bonn area, the upper Rhine region, central Belgium and the Paris region. In Eastern Europe, Budapest and a wide area of Poland — including such major industrial cities as Warsaw, Gdansk, Poznan, Wroclaw, Katowice and Krakow — all showed big gains. Throughout Europe's industrial heartland, growth was based on a mixture of still-expanding manufacturing industries such as engineering, electrical engineering and chemicals, and higher-level urban service industries. On the other hand, the areas of slow growth or decline tend to have been in rural regions, peripheral to the major centres of population in their respective countries, and sometimes also peripheral in relation to Europe generally — a contrast with recent American experience.

Further — and in complete contradiction of the American trends — in many parts of Europe the larger urban regions have continued to grow rapidly. This is true for instance of Germany, where much of the growth has gone into medium-sized metropolitan areas with between 300,000 and 1 million people, and of Italy and Spain, where it has concentrated into some of the biggest metropolitan areas within the national settlement systems.

The main causal explanation of these trends has already been noticed: it is mass rural-to-urban migration. Rationalisation of peasant agriculture, still far from complete in many European countries in the mid-1970s, produced large rural surplus populations. Local cities were unable in many cases to absorb all this surplus, so that longer-distance migration streams — inter-regional and indeed international — came into being, feeding the larger urban centres which were the main locations of fast-growing manufacturing industry. The main beneficiaries were the central cities, hence the tendency to centralisation in the 1950s. In most of Europe, after 1960, (after 1970 in Southern Europe) a counter-stream developed from central cores to suburban rings. All this suggests a fairly steady progression over time, from centralisation to decentralisation, and eventually to decline of the largest urban systems.

The question must be, how far away this final stage is. Migration trends changed sharply after 1970. Before then there was strong migration from peripheral regions into the more heavily-urbanised and densely-populated regions, including Paris, the Rhone axis and Marseilles, the lower Rhine and the Munich area, and Brussels. But after 1970 only three of these areas (Lyons, Marseilles and Munich) continued to show migration gains. However, this did not represent a process of 'counter-urbanisation' so much as a combination of three factors: a return of foreign guest workers, an out-migration of older retired people (while workers still migrated in) and a relative lack of employment opportunities because of the economic recession (Koch 1980, 60-3). Therefore, the long-term evolution is still in doubt.

In any event, down to the mid-1970s most of Europe was not suffering from the Anglo-American syndrome of inner urban decline. The Tri-National Inner Cities project, in 1978-9, discovered that 'problems of decline in German cities are still not generally recognised' (Davies 1980, 1). There is some strong and carefully documented evidence that decline is affecting the four largest cities of Randstad Holland (Amsterdam, The Hague, Rijnmond, Utrecht), where rapid core-to-ring decentralisation is occurring (Ayodeji and Vonk 1980, 100). Indeed, by the early 1970s the metropolitan cores as a whole were showing slight decline as compared with the very rapid growth of the inner rings (Ayodeji and Vonk 1980, 93). This is not surprising, as other evidence suggests that the Netherlands and Belgium were probably the first countries on the European mainland to demonstrate decentralisation, as early as the 1950s (Hall and Hay 1980, 116). Elsewhere in Europe, one should not expect to find such pronounced trends.

The Japanese Experience

In other parts of the advanced industrial world, it seems that deconcentration may be becoming the order of the day. Thus in Japan (Glickman 1978, Chapter 2) metropolitan areas began to decentralise overall, from cores to rings, during the 1960s. This, however, was a process mainly affecting the largest metropolitan areas — Tokyo, Osaka and Nagasaki — which were continuing to grow very rapidly even during the 1970s. Smaller metropolitan areas continued to centralise overall, as people still poured into their core cities. But Glickman did find some evidence of convergence between Japan and the west: the slowing-down in the rate of increase of the largest metropolitan areas, the absolute losses of population from the largest central cities, the growth of medium-sized cities near to major centres, and even of medium-sized cities in more rural areas, all suggest that Japan is tending closer to the United States and Britain on the continuum of industrialisation-urbanisation (Glickman 1978, Chapter 3).

We can conclude that the two processes, industrialisation and urbanisation, are closely linked. Britain and the United States are de-urbanising and they appear also to be de-industrialising — at least in certain regions. The two processes are however not identical; and there is no necessary causal relationship. It is clear, however, that among other countries down to the mid-1970s only the United States truly demonstrated a phenomenon of inner city decline, sufficiently marked to be labelled a major problem requiring a policy solution. For that reason, it is relevant to go on and look in more detail both at the problem as perceived there, and at successive attempts to find a solution to it. This is the burden of Chapter 5.

5　The American Experience

Richard Kirwan

There are two justifications for this sideways look at the United States — despite the fact that it delays the return to our primary British concerns. One is that America has a great wealth of material describing and analysing trends and policies. The other is that the United States seems to share similar trends of urban change; indeed, in this regard — as just seen in Chapter 4 — Britain seems tò be more like the United States than anywhere else. So it should be useful to ask three questions. First, how far does this apparent similarity stand up to more detailed examination? Secondly, what are the possible explanations for the American trends and how far do they accord with British analysis? And third, to what extent do American policy initiatives point to new possibilities on this side of the Atlantic?

We have to start with a caveat about the data. Exactly comparable data do not exist for the two countries. There are differences in definitions, in criteria, and in statistical practice. To take one example: American urban data refer to Standard Metropolitan Statistical Areas (SMBAs), and to central cities within them. These latter frequently provide the best approximation to the 'inner city' under discussion in this book. But they refer to administrative units, the extent of which inevitably varies from one place to another. And, while the British 'metropolitan areas' analysed in Chapter 2 have been defined so as to correspond closely to their American counterparts, neither they nor their 'central cores' can do so exactly. They are merely the best possible proxy for a broad overview. A better definition of the 'inner city' in the American context, as Berry (1980, 10) points out, might be that area constructed before the Great Depression of the 1930s. But in younger cities in the south and west, even that definition might not be adequate.

[1] This chapter was edited by Peter Hall from an earlier draft by Richard Kirwan, based mainly on material in his working paper: Kirwan (1980a), *The Inner City in Context*, Paper 8.

The fact is that all generalisations of this kind are subject to exceptions. So the conclusions must be treated with caution.

Demographic Trends

The decline of the American central city has been dramatic. In 1950, 35.5 percent of the American population — then 151 million — lived in the central cities of SMSAs. By 1976, the total population had increased to 215 million, the number of SMSAs had increased to 272 but the proportion living in their central cities had fallen to 28.8 percent. Since 1970, in fact, the total population of the central cities has been falling at a rate of 0.6 percent annually. But the steady decline in the average size of households, from 3.37 in 1950 down to an estimated 2.89 in 1976, has meant that the same numbers of households were to be found throughout metropolitan areas at the two dates.

This population shift has four main components. First, long-distance migration has taken millions away from the north and west and into the south and west — and in these latter regions, the populations of SMSAs have been further swelled by the influx of Mexican (many illegal) and Asian immigrants. Second, outward population movements have caused central cities to decline and suburban rings to grow — though more recently, even the growth in the rings has slowed while non-metropolitan areas have shown sudden surges. Third, and a cause of the second, central cities have experienced migration losses while suburbs and outer areas have received in-migrants — though in fact, only a minority of the overall gains and losses represent actual moves within the metropolitan area. These trends are similar to those observed for Britain in Chapter 2. Fourth, during the 1960s the falling birth rates in the central cities masked to some extent the effects of out-migration. But by the 1970s the falling birth rate had spread also to the central cities, and the effects of out-migration became evident. This history seems to have been different from that in Britain, where the decline in birth rate seems to have affected the central city earlier than the rest of the urban system — a product of selective out-migration.

In America as in Britain, population loss from central cities has left people and places with severe economic problems and without resources to meet them. Yet migration has been a much greater force in the United States, leading to the process labelled by Brian Berry as 'counter-urbanisation' (Berry 1976, 17): a growth in almost undeveloped areas, as well as at the very periphery of the urban systems. The British-American contrast, in other words, is between deconcentration and de-urbanisation.

Another potent American-British distinction concerns the role of ethnic mix. During the 1950s, migration brought large numbers of blacks from the south into the central cities of the north and east. During the 1960s, this effect was amplified by large out-movements of whites from these same cities. Only very recently, in the 1970s, has there been a marked increase in black migration into the suburbs. The resulting black concentrations in the cities are on a scale unparalleled in Britain. Thus in 1971, only a handful of British core areas had 10 percent or more of their populations born in the New Commonwealth or to parents of New Commonwealth origin. But in 1970 in the United States, blacks constituted more than one-third of the population in no less than 25 cities of over 100,000 inhabitants, and no less than 71 percent of the population of Washington DC. More recent is the growth of the Spanish-speaking groups, which now comprise about 9.5 percent of the entire population of all central cities. Two-thirds are of Mexican origin and about one-third from Puerto Rico and Cuba. So the role of race and ethnicity is vastly greater than in British cities — despite British media publicity on the subject.

Labour and Employment

The 'baby boom' of the 1950s has now worked its way through to the 20-25 age group, and in the 1980s the numbers in the working age groups can be expected to decline. But this process, which has been happening for some time, has been more than offset by a rise in the overall percentage working or seeking employment — a function of the increase in female employment. In the future, with most adults working, there will be a rise in household income, but a fall in the time available for other activities — pointing to increased domestic investment in labour-saving devices, with clear implications for design of housing. Associated with this shift is a changing locus of residential preference. Traditionally, suburbs have been regarded as good places for raising children, but as the baby boom generation move into adulthood they are demonstrating low fertility — a fact that may favour central-city living once again.

Throughout the United States, the most rapidly expanding employment sectors since the mid-1960s have been — as in Britain — services, finance and government (excluding defence). There has been a severe fall in manufacturing and construction in the older industrial areas of the north and east, and below-average expansion there in the growing service sectors. In the south and west, conversely, most sectors have shown expansion. These trends are strikingly reflected in the employment records of the cities. Northern cities have fared worst than southern and western ones; large cities have fared worse than small ones. Manufacturing jobs in northeastern cities grew — albeit more slowly than elsewhere — down to 1965; thereafter they contracted. Continuation of this pattern will increasingly attract industry away from its traditional locations — a pattern that strikingly parallels British concerns.

The causes, too, are similar: low transportation costs, cheap land and low wages have all helped to attract employment away from the older manufacturing cities and into smaller places in previously unindustrialised areas. As Berry (1980, 18) notes: 'Developments in transportation and communication have made it possible for each generation to live further away from activity centres, for these activity centres to disperse, and for information users to rely upon information sources that are spatially more distant . . . In other words, large, dense urban concentrations are no longer necessary for external economies to be present'. Equally significant has been a change in the distribution of service industry, which has paralleled the deconcentration of manufacturing and has thus amplified its effects.

As in Britain, so in the United States, there has been recent concern that the rise in unemployment has been heavily concentrated among school-leavers, women and minority groups. The concentration of declining industries and minority groups in the central cities generates much higher levels of unemployment there than elsewhere. Also reflecting unemployment and lack of wage earners, family incomes in central cities tend to be low — even though, for those that have jobs, wages in northern cities remain higher than in the expanding cities of the south.

Housing

America, like Britain, has seen a steady advance in owner-occupation — but the United States is further along the road, with 69 percent of the stock owner-occupied in 1970, and 75 percent in 1975, compared with about 53 percent in Britain in 1978. The movement surged after World War Two, mainly because of the effective introduction of tax subsidies for home ownership, but also as a consequence of the opening up of the suburbs through highway construction, coupled with growth of household income. These forces massively encouraged low-density, single-family living patterns on the urban fringe, and — as Berry has argued — triggered inner city depopulation. For, between 1963 and 1976, households expanded only by 17 millions yet no less than 27 million new housing units were built. The result — quite unlike Britain,

which still has a massive problem of obsolescence of its housing stock —
is that, on the whole, Americans have been able simply to abandon
their older housing, which is of course concentrated in the central cities
(Berry 1980, 16).

As the urban boundary has been pushed outward, so there has been
faster removal or abandonment of the older central city housing. As
Berry puts it, 'what are being abandoned are those environments that
were crucial in the traditional metropolis-driven growth process; the
high-density, congested face-to-face central city settings that are now
being perceived as ageing, polluted, and crime-ridden with declining
services and employment bases, and escalating taxes' (Berry 1980, 18).
Thus the great majority of Americans live in good housing conditions,
while substandard housing is now concentrated in relatively small
pockets in central cities: a marked contrast to Britain, where public
renewal has removed the worst of the urban housing stock, and where
substandard housing is now scattered fairly widely through the urban
system.

As Berry puts it, American 'housing policy has been *de facto* the
only national policy for urban development' (Berry 1980, 17). Unlike
its British parallel, it has never included a very substantial element of
public-subsidised housing. Federally-financed programmes of rehabilitation, which expanded very rapidly around 1970, were allowed to
contract severely in the mid-1970s. To compensate in part, there has
recently been a steady growth in the volume of unsubsidised private rehabilitation of the older housing stock in the cities. And, with inflation
plus recession in the second half of the 1970s, new housing starts have
fallen. The fixed interest mortgage system, common in the United
States until inflation eroded it in the late 1970s, provided a powerful
financial incentive for the upgrading of the existing stock of housing
while capital was tight, making 'the home repair industry one of the
strongest counter-cyclical sectors in the American economy' (Berry
1980, 20).

Demographic and social trends, too, have contributed to this
process. Increasing opportunities for women in well-paid professional
employment, and the simultaneous decline in fertility, have undoubtedly been a major factor in the move to rehabilitate older central city
housing. Certainly, small households have grown in number in central
cities, and a principal cause has been the expansion of the childless —
and even non-family — small household among the young adult population there. Another has been the presence of a significant cluster of professional jobs supporting a young, college-educated labour force. This

suggests that revitalisation on a significant scale may be limited to the major metropolitan cities, which alone have the necessary concentration of post-industrial management, control and information-processing activities.

Certainly, despite the general and continuing spread of owner-occupation, the percentage of owner-occupied dwellings in central cities has recently grown only slowly. Moreover, despite the continuing exodus of population, central city housing markets have not eased: vacancy rates have hardly increased and, indeed, in the important rented sector they have marginally worsened. The most probable reason is abandonment, which in the 1970s grew to massive proportions in certain cities, notably St Louis, New York, and — to a lesser extent — Philadelphia, Chicago, Cleveland, Boston and elsewhere. In New York City, for instance, it is estimated that between 1969 and 1978 no less than 89,000 units were abandoned. Thus the paradox may exist that the metropolitan areas with the lowest rates of replacement supply may be those in which the inflation of housing costs is greatest and the pace of neighbourhood revitalisation is most rapid.

The obvious negative side of this process of rejuvenation is that it displaces the poorer households in the rental sector — predominantly the old and minority groups. They either try to stay in the neighbourhood at higher rents, or move to other deteriorated neighbourhoods that are not subject to the same pressures. Thus the total housing stock available to the poor may be shrinking, as they are squeezed between reduced rates of new building at one end and the pressures of the childless multi-earning middle-class household at the other.

Metropolitan Fiscal Affairs

As in Britain, the period since 1950 has witnessed continuous and rapid growth of government expenditure, especially at the local level. But the differences are very wide. Only in recent years have American local governments become significant beneficiaries of central funding, as priorities have shifted away from highways and towards welfare and education — a sharp contrast with Britain, where for years local governments have enjoyed substantial central support. As compared with Britain, then, local finance is more diverse, and consequently harder to describe generally. But it can be said that at the heart of the urban fiscal problem lie three processes: a much slower growth of the tax base in declining cities, as compared with growing ones; a widening disparity within metropolitan areas, between the fiscal position of the central cities and of their suburbs; and a changing distribution of aid as between local governments.

Until the late 1960s, it generally remained true that — despite the 'flight to the suburbs' and other forms of outmigration — the taxable capacity of the central cities remained superior to that of the suburbs. But since then, their situation has deteriorated. And this is only half the story, for — as generally admitted — the 'needs' of central cities are much greater than that of the suburbs. In addition, the cities have faced sharp increases in costs since the mid-1960s, due in part to a rapid increase in local labour costs in municipal employment following increased Federal support and powerful union bargaining, in part to inflation and rising debt service charges, and in part to increased pension obligations. Between 1972 and 1976 alone, the real purchasing power of the revenue base of all municipalities and counties fell by between 5 and 7 percent — while the monetary value of the dollar fell by more than 36 percent.

Just as in Britain, the gap between needs and revenues has been followed by an extremely rapid growth in the cities' dependence on central funds. By 1978, direct Federal aid is estimated to have risen to over 78 percent of local revenues in Detroit and Buffalo and to over 50 percent in St Louis, Newark, Cleveland and Philadelphia. Although this is still a much smaller central percentage than the overall central government contribution to local expenditure in Britain, by historical standards it represents a massive change in Federal-local relations, for as recently as the late 1960s Federal funding to most cities amounted to less than 5 percent of revenues. Nevertheless, the American cities have a much more serious fiscal problem than British ones, where the rate support grant system has continued to work reasonably well. American experience thus shows what can happen to a country that retains a high degree of autonomy in local fiscal affairs (Kirwan 1980b, 74).

Explanations

As the trends of urban development have shifted, so has American perception of the inner city question. In the late 1950s, it was seen as a counterpart to the process of suburbanisation that was then the dominant trend. A number of studies related this to the changing balance of power in state and metropolitan affairs: the growing movement out of inner cities was attributed in part to the desire to reassert political control over local affairs. Other analyses related inner city depopulation to a rapidly changing pattern of accessibility, with major effects on the land market and on opportunities for residential location.

By the mid-1960s, the changes were seen to be even deeper, affecting the whole pattern of the economy. The employment and economic base of the inner cities was weakening, and this was explained in terms of four main factors: first, changes in productive processes necessitating large sites and single-storey manufacturing plants; second, abandonment of rail transport in favour of the new interstate and circumferential highways, and the consequent movement towards highway interchanges; third, the effect of the outward population movement on the location of commercial activity; and fourth, the movement to the suburbs of the skilled labour force, coupled with the presence there of 'captive', largely female labour for light industrial and service activities.

At the same time, inner city black communities emerged for the first time as a strong force in national policies, while research began to show just how important the racial dimension was to the employment and housing conditions of the largely black and Hispanic residents of many of these areas. Two opposed conceptions emerged of the possible role of the American city — to be mirrored subsequently, in a less starkly-drawn way, in Britain. One approach stressed the inner city as a stronghold of minority power, heavily dependent upon Federal assistance, and using predominantly political leverage to obtain a fair share of employment and housing opportunities, with strong community control over economic development. The other saw the inner city as still an integral part of an extended economic system, with equality of opportunity for minorities extended through anti-discrimination measures, assisted dispersal of low-income housing and transport improvements that would give inner city residents better access to suburban jobs. But the undeniable reality was that the inner city was becoming increasingly dependent upon Federal funding — and this directed attention to issues of public finance.

Towards the end of the 1960s, these contraposed views each took a slightly different stance. The integrationist view pointed to the experience of rapid economic growth over much of the decade — partly, it is true, engendered by military expenditure — and suggested that the American economy was now entering a 'post-industrial' phase, in which the future of the inner city would depend on its ability to attract the burgeoning tertiary sector of the economy and on the ability of its population to respond to the demands for labour for this sector. The activist view was heavily influenced by the turmoil surrounding the anti-war movement, the student protests and the emergence of minorities as a powerful political force. Thus emerged a series of more radical, Marxist-leaning conceptualisations of the inner city question, focusing on the primacy of class struggle and on the relationship of the inner city problem to national and international economic processes. At the same time, as economic conditions worsened in the 1970s, the inner cities became even more dependent on the public and especially the Federal sector, giving added point to the fiscal analysis of their problems. By the early 1980s, in consequence, interpretations of the inner city problem can be seen to have polarised much more sharply than hitherto.

Two schools of analysis

On the one hand, there is a structuralist or Marxist style of analysis; on the other, a school that reflects natural processes and market forces of adjustment. The distinction reflects not so much the treatment of the problem itself, but rather a fundamental difference in the theoretical approach to the facts.

Within the structuralist camp, there are many different perspectives. Some stress long-term problems of adjustment to the 'long cycles' of capitalism, following the work of the Soviet economist Kondratieff in the 1920s (Kondratieff 1935 (1925)). This is an interest increasingly shared by non-Marxist economists (Rostow 1977, 83-103). Some concentrate on the process of industrial restructuring and in particular on the shift of manufacturing from the north to the south, which is seen as part of a general strategic response to declining profits and increasingly hard international competition, compelling a de-skilling of the labour force and a separation of production and control functions. (This kind of analysis is very close to a parallel British movement, already outlined in Chapter 2.) One variant sees the shift in terms of the lower public service levels of the southern cities, which arise from historically different political sources there; the implicit suggestion is that lower local taxes may prove attractive to footloose large corporations (Lupsha and Siembieda 1977, 184-7). Others stress the conflict between the increasing subsidies necessary to support investment in declining metropolitan areas, and the loss of fiscal capacity there; and the parallel conflict between the attempt to increase the tax base through central redevelopment and highway construction, and the wholesale physical destruction and social dislocation that invariably accompany such a policy.

In contrast, the other school of analysis stresses not so much the problem, as the success — or failure — of adjustment to changing conditions. Its model is essentially unchanged from that of the 1960s: it emphasises the role of locational preferences in the decisions of households to move, the declining significance of freight costs and the prime importance of labour supply for the location of manufacturing industry, and the increasing importance of the tertiary sector and the investments that are made in new office and commercial centres. The inner city is perceived to be threatened by major external forces — world recession, internal competition, energy costs and the like. Here, there is some agreement with the structuralists, but the lesson to be drawn is different: it is that cities must adjust to changing circumstances, by ingenuity and above all by flexibility. The failures, in many cases so far, are attributed to lack of these qualities, to rigidities in the land and housing markets — as in the case of rent control in New York City and now in other cities — and to failures of policy response. A wise policy, in this view, and one that would be realistic, would ease the decline of urban areas past reclaim, while supporting and upgrading viable neighbourhoods by encouraging the presence there of young, highly educated, affluent households. These would move in and spontaneously upgrade some areas, while lower-income people — especially the minorities — would be encouraged to move out in search of better housing than they now enjoy, for instance in the older suburbs outside the central cities. Thus the key to success would lie in getting the market to work again, to the mutual benefit of every income group.

American Policy Initiatives

To try and meet the growing problems of American inner cities, over the last twenty years a large number of policy initiatives have been developed. The origins lie in the Great Society programmes, launched by the Johnson administration in the second half of the 1960s. The main programmes specifically aimed at the cities at that time were Model Cities and some of the Economic Opportunity programme. But the cities benefited also from the massive increase in Federal spending on a wide variety of social programmes, including pensions, unemployment insurance, aid to dependent families, health, medical aid and education. Urban public transport also began to receive large-scale Federal aid, though this was not always used to help the inner city.

Economically, few of the Johnson programmes had lasting impact. The practical effect was more political in nature: it was to alert and galvanise the poor and predominantly black populations of the inner cities so that they played a significant role in local policies and in

demanding a larger share of Federal resources. The Model Cities programme epitomises the shortcomings of policy in that era: ambitious in
character, in many ways well-conceived, it suffered from inadequate
funding (especially after the costs of the Vietnam war began to mount),
from local controversy and corruption, and from the inexperience and
inability of the Federal bureaucracy in the management of so large a
programme.

Under the Nixon presidency, the most important development was
undoubtedly the reorganisation of the Federal funding system, through
the introduction of general revenue-sharing and the rolling-up of previous programmes into the various special revenue-sharing programmes.
Ironically, the initial intention was to divert funds away from the major
cities. Yet the programme established a mechanism for redistribution,
which, in the period of recession after the oil crisis of 1974, became the
main source of assistance to large central cities. This was fortified by
changes in 1976 to the formula for distribution of the new Community
Block Grant to reflect unemployment, the age of the housing stock,
low rates of population and income growth, and employment losses in
manufacturing and retailing — all of which tended to direct the major
emphasis toward the distressed cities of the north and east.

By the middle of the Carter administration, in early 1978, inner
urban policies in the United States had been progressively shaped into a
number of separate lines. General revenue sharing gave general fiscal
assistance. It was supplemented by Community Development Block
Grant, giving assistance for land acquisition, for acquisition, construct-
tion and renewal of industrial and commercial facilities, for open space
and neighbourhood facilities and for planning, housing, rehabilitation
historic preservation. Further supplementation came from the Urban
Development Action Grant, which provided funds to 'leverage' private
investment in revitalisation projects. Funding under the Comprehensive
Employment Training Act aided manpower training, job creation,
youth employment initiatives, public employment and similar schemes.
Public Works Employment Act and Employment Development Act
grants, as their names indicated, helped the creation of local jobs. The
Anti-Recession Assistance Act provided specific revenue-sharing funds,
while there were miscellaneous categorical programmes for water and
sewerage, transportation and housing. Additionally, many major social
programmes (assistance to families, medical care) and general instruments of economic stimulus (such as the Small Business Administration
programme) made a significant contribution to the overall level of inner
city prosperity.

The long-awaited announcement of President Carter's urban policy, during 1978, added little to this well-established bundle of programmes. (Indeed, the details were rapidly overshadowed by the administration's desperate decision to cut economic and social programmes in its campaign to reduce inflation and strengthen the dollar.) Based on the concept of 'partnership', the main proposals were limited to four main themes: improved inter-governmental coordination; restructured Federal assistance programmes to replace anti-recession revenue-sharing; new employment and economic development measures including grants and tax credits; and expansion of housing and community development programmes, including additional low-interest loan finance for rehabilitation schemes. Nothing in this package represents a radical departure from the thinking of previous administrations; nor does it answer any of the major controversies about the objectives or the form of policy. Unsurprisingly, many observers — especially black ones — remained sceptical about the likely effectiveness of the Carter policy.

Lessons to be learned

American inner city policies offer much valuable experience, both as to the causes and effects of inner city change, and as to the capacities and limitations of policy in influencing that change. To be sure, the object lessons stem rather more from the failures than from the successes. As the evolution of Carter's urban policy makes clear, there has recently been a deep uncertainty — if not actual despair — about the direction that American inner city policy should take. For it would not be unfair to say that almost everything has been tried and that nothing has succeeded. Physical development was the central theme of the urban renewal period of the 1950s and early 1960s. This had disastrous social effects for the inner city poor. Income transfers were expanded greatly in the 1960s. Though they led to some improvement in housing conditions, they had little impact on the underlying problems. Service delivery was another major theme of that period — and in the Model Cities programme, it was carefully integrated with physical renewal. But, because of lack of funds, the impact was limited. The same goes for the New Towns in Town programme.

Similarly, many different kinds of implementation have been tried and then discredited. Urban renewal used Federal funds but relied heavily on the private development industry; it created private wealth and social disruption, and was justifiably attacked. Model Cities and other Great Society programmes required Federal administration of local implementation efforts; the machinery was not equal to the task,

and there were many criticisms of misuse of funds. These same programmes also provided a role for community organisations to create
and administer their own programmes, but once again there was
evidence of widespread corruption and misappropriation of funding.
New Towns in Town revived the concept of autonomous public-private
corporations, but the most celebrated example — the Urban Development Corporation of New York — was also quickly embroiled in a
financial and administrative scandal. More recently, special revenue
sharing funds have gone to cities to carry out their own programmes,
but the result, according to critics, is that the cities have used them to
finance initiatives that they would have undertaken anyway, so as to be
able to undertake other projects or reduce their tax rates.

At the local level, the recent emphasis on job creation and business
stimulation has generated a wide variety of different initiatives in different cities, but there is little evidence that the incentives are working,
and legitimate concern is expressed that they set-off unproductive
competition between cities. More importantly, any gains from new
private investment have been overshadowed by losses in the public
sector from local fiscal cuts and by rising national unemployment.
Moreover, labour costs in the cities remain high despite serious unemployment, so they lack a competitive attraction to new enterprise.

Underlying these concerns remain the same major unresolved issues
that — as we already saw in Chapter 3 and shall see in Chapter 5 — also
recur in the British context. Should a revitalisation strategy be predominantly people-oriented or predominantly place-oriented? Should
the major objective be to expand the tax base so as to allow cities to
undertake much-needed programmes, or will this merely provide an
excuse to permit downtown redevelopment and expansion and to keep
taxes down, with no impact on the areas of real need? At what level
should public expenditure be targeted, and how far is a selective
approach to neighbourhood improvement economically justified or
politically feasible?

The Relevance for Britain

Clearly, there are many strong resemblances between the American and
the British experience of the inner city problem. We cannot fail to learn
from the American process of change and from the policy responses to
it. But that does not mean that every detail of the process, and every
policy initiative, is equally relevant. The United States has very different economic, political and institutional structures and traditions from

Britain. The day-to-day reality of policy and practice reveals striking differences.

Nevertheless, the common experiences can tell us a great deal about the causes and effects of inner city change and about the limitations of policy. In the late 1970s, both countries have faced an accelerated decline of their inner cities, as part of a general crisis in the advanced capitalist countries. As centres of production, the inner cities of the older metropolitan areas are the victims of a radical restructuring of manufacturing industry, which the change in international competitive conditions has stirred. As zones of potentially profitable land development, they become victims of the developers' need to respond to rising inflation and interest rates by concentrating development in areas of high-intensity, low-risk investment. In these regards, Britain and the United States face the same structural conditions. And to a significant extent, the ability of their governments to respond to inner city needs is constrained by the same macroeconomic circumstances and by a similar ideological approach to economic policy. So there are many similarities.

But equally, there are great differences. Britain has not experienced the same local fiscal crisis that has dominated the American urban debate of the 1970s, because it did not share the deliberate devolution of central control that was inaugurated under Nixon's new Federalism. On the contrary, its central government has sought deliberately to cushion its cities against the direct fiscal consequences of the general economic crisis. Thus in Britain the main effects of the crisis have been absorbed nationally, while in the United States the resulting series of local fiscal crises has represented a serious political threat to the stability of local political systems. Conversely, Britain has no real equivalent of the 'boom' areas like Texas and Southern California – though some of the medium-sized towns of southern England provide a minor parallel – so that the politics of urban decline are not bound up in the same way with the belief in the freedom of the entrepreneur to exploit his opportunities anywhere he thinks fit. The drift of the more affluent professional households back to the inner city began significantly to affect lower-income housing opportunities rather earlier in the United States than in Britain, and for rather different reasons. The United States had no real equivalent to the containment policies that affected the location of workplaces and residential areas in and around British cities – though recently, environmental and growth controls have begun to have similar effects there also. On the other hand, Britain has no equivalent to the widespread abandonment and resulting desolaation in American inner city areas, largely because the public sector has remained a willing buyer of inner city land. And perhaps most important of all, there is no real equivalent in Britain to the racial factor as it affects American urban policies in virtually every major declining city.

Not surprisingly, therefore, the machinery of government policy also differs significantly. Even if the two countries share common intents and programmes — for job creation, for housing rehabilitation, for public service delivery — the details of American policies are so closely geared to their own structure of inter-governmental relations and their traditions of government that they may be difficult to apply in Britain. To take one example: America shows a greater willingness to use public funds to support voluntary, ethnic and community initiatives in inner city neighbourhoods. But this is not merely a convenient response to a period of tight budgets; it also reflects a long tradition in the American political system. Perhaps, though, there is a convergence over time; for at least some of the British inner city partnership and programme areas, since 1977, have similarly brought together public, private and voluntary initiatives in a useful way, and — as we shall see in the following chapter — this tendency is if anything on the increase, with strong government encouragement.

Britain, on the other hand, has at its disposal a number of policy initiatives that — *prima facie* at least — should give it an advantage: a more sophisticated system of fiscal assistance to cities, through the Rate Support Grant and associated funding systems; a well-established system of public housing, that is better able to protect low-income households against adverse market conditions; a more extensive and effective set of instruments to influence industrial location, through the Industrial Development Certificate procedure coupled with regional incentives; and finally, a more extensive system of metropolitan government, with stronger centrally-directed powers to control suburban expansion. One might conclude from the American experience that Britain would be foolish to abandon any of these potentially useful devices — though some, such as the IDC procedures, were greatly weakened at the end of the 1970s. But equally, one would be rash to conclude that in consequence inner city conditions will remain significantly better in Britain than in the United States. Some of the British successes may be more apparent than real — as the very limited achievements of metropolitan government will illustrate.

What is clear is that there is no magic American inner city policy that could achieve dramatic effects if transferred to Britain. By now, both countries have pretty well tried every possibility that their dominant ideology permits. Even where policies are similar in general conception, the detailed differences in government and in local political, social, cultural and economic history will make for very different applications. So policy comparisons may prove fruitless.

There are however some possible lines that might prove fruitful. One is to try to harness community action and involvement, especially through locally and ethnically based businesses, in implementing local development programmes. Another is to try to develop a system of Urban Impact Analysis to assess the effects on the inner cities of policy proposals not only within the narrow field of urban policy, but more widely across the whole field of economic and social policy. A third is to try to assess the longer-term implications – especially the longer-term costs – of the neglect of the infrastructure of the inner cities, which is so evident in both countries because of the present economic crisis. And a fourth is to try to obtain a greater degree of cooperation from voluntary organisations together with the public and the private sectors, as indeed is now occurring in some inner city partnerships and programmes.

Some Unanswered Questions

Underlying all what has just been said there is a basic need for more understanding of processes. In both countries, we need to comprehend better the structural changes that are occurring in the organisation of both manufacturing and service industries, and in the process of land development and the organisation of urban real estate. Better understanding of these processes will be crucial in predicting the very different world that will be faced by both countries in the 1980s – and so for developing policy responses to them. Otherwise, as has happened too often in the past, ill-conceived policies will consume all too many resources and will have all too little impact.

Beyond that, the unanswered questions for British researchers are those that have just been discussed in evaluating the American experience for Britons. Though we should beware of too facile a belief in transferring policy solutions across oceans and cultures, there is room for further evaluation of some American efforts, particularly in harnessing voluntary initiatives. A good beginning has been made in the Tri-National Inner Cities study (Davies 1980), but there is probably more to be learned. Certainly, the considerable volume of American work on urban impact analysis (Glickman (ed.) 1980, Glickman (ed.) 1981) calls for evaluation and review in a British context. The American experience may be chastening for British policy-makers, but there are positive lessons to be learned as well as negative ones.

6 British Policy Responses

Susan Laurence and Peter Hall

This chapter returns to Britain. It tries to describe, analyse and evaluate the government's response to the perceived problem of the inner city between the mid-1960s and the start of the 1980s. It has to be a tentative attempt, because so many of the most important policy initiatives — above all the inner city partnerships and programmes — are still in the middle of implementation. It also has to be fairly summary, for obvious reasons of space. The chapter draws on some recent evaluations (Wick 1977; Edwards and Batley 1978; Lawless 1979; McKay and Cox 1979a,b) that treat the policies in greater detail than is possible here.

The main aim is to take up from previous chapters, and to ask: how did politicians and other decision-makers perceive the problem? How far did research contribute to their perception? What was the relationship between research findings, perceptions and policy prescriptions? How did the actors then monitor the progress of their policies? Did they commission further research to that end — and if so, what were the findings? Did they in turn contribute to a redefinition of the problem, and if so in what way? Was that in turn reflected in a policy shift, and if so of what kind? To anticipate the chapter's findings, we shall find that indeed research did contribute to a redefinition, and that that in turn was followed by a major policy shift — but with precisely what outcome, it is difficult at the time of writing to say.

In the period in question there was a positive proliferation of inner city-related programmes that followed hard on each other, indeed often overlapping: the Education Priority Areas, the Urban Programme, the Community Development Projects, the experiments in Area Management and Neighbourhood Representation, the Transmitted Deprivation studies, the Comprehensive Community Programmes, the Inner Area studies, the Inner City Partnerships and Programmes, the Urban Development Corporations and — not formally part of inner city policies, but certainly of relevance to them — the Enterprise Zones. We cannot hope to give equal space to each; rather, we shall concentrate on those generally regarded as most significant.

First, directly taking up the theme of the previous chapter, we look at the specific influence of American thinking on early British policy ideas in the middle 1960s. Then we describe, in chronological order, the development of the main initiatives. We then seek to analyse them collectively, according to their underlying social assumptions, their objectives, and their methodology. Lastly, we make a general evaluation of their relevance and significance.

The American Influence

An important influence — though certainly not the only one — in generating inner city policy initiatives was undoubtedly the experience of the United States. During the second half of the 1960s, the major thrust in American policies came from the so-called Great Society Programs of the Johnson administration. Of the initiatives loosely gathered under this heading, only the Economic Opportunity Programs and the Model Cities Programs were specifically aimed at urban problems. But at least as important in total impact on the cities was the whole package of social measures that were introduced by the administration.

The Community Development Programmes — introduced under the auspices of the Office of Economic Opportunity through the 1964 Economic Opportunity Act — became the target of particularly vehement criticism. It was unclear — so the critics said — whether they were intended to coordinate existing initiatives, or to mobilise the poor, or to provide new and much-needed services — or even simply to promote Johnson's re-election (Moynihan 1966). The Model Cities programme, set up in 1966 in order to link public spending with urban renewal and environmental rehabilitation, with the provision of social services and the provision of low and middle-income housing, encountered equally fierce criticism, though on almost opposite grounds: that it set very high standards — perhaps incapable of achievement — for implementation on the part of local authorities. It failed finally because of a squeeze on funds, brought about in large measure by the Vietnam war, coupled with the inability of the Federal bureaucracy to manage such a large and complex programme.

But the main effect of the urban programmes must be judged more on social and political criteria: on their capacity to alert and galvanise the poor, black population of the inner cities to demand their rightful share of welfare programmes (Kirwan 1980a; Piven 1974). Perhaps, if

British politicians and officials had been better aware of both the failures and the programmes' major thrusts, they would have been less enthusiastic than they became – and almost certainly, they would not have embarked on the Community Development Programmes (Higgens 1978). It may be true, though, that American reports of the problems involved in working with grassroots organisations caused the British to rely largely on government initiatives – though traditional civil service caution may also have been at work, of course. Be that as it may, the most influential American programmes were Headstart, which inspired the British Educational Priority Areas, and the Community Action Program, which inspired the British Urban Aid and Community Development project package.

Discovery of the Problem

Policies for defined local areas, usually small in size and designed to combat concentrations of local problems, were by no means new to Britain in the mid-1960s. The model can be traced back to the slum clearance areas of the 1930s, to the Comprehensive Development Areas designated under the 1947 Town and Country Planning Act, to the Clean Air zones designated under the 1956 Act and to the Conservation Areas which were introduced in the Civic Amenities Act of 1968. Outside the legislative sphere, the Buchanan report of 1963 had proposed 'environmental areas' to cope with the impact of traffic; while the Milner Holland report on London rented housing, in 1965, had called for 'areas of special control', where poor living conditions could be attacked comprehensively. This last approach was implemented in legislation through the Housing Act of 1969, which provided for the creation by local authorities of General Improvement Areas.

What was most interesting about the early inner city initiatives, however, was that they defined areas of need not in terms of physical decay, but in terms of economic and social characteristics. First were the provisions of Section 11 of the 1966 Local Government Act for special aid in areas of concentration of Commonwealth immigrants. These were closely followed by the Educational Priority Areas scheme, which was based on recommendations in the Plowden report on primary education of 1967. It broke new ground by using socio-economic indicators to try to identify areas of need. But the main impetus to intervention at that time was not so much the analytical studies – which tended to follow rather than to procede the initiatives – as the political storms generated around Commonwealth immigration. These followed publication of the 1966 Census, which showed that the non-white population appeared to have grown since 1951 from 75,000 to 595,000, and Enoch Powell's 'rivers of blood' speech of April 1968. The Urban Programme, announced with great publicity only two weeks after this speech, was clearly an attempt to defuse its impact by demonstrating positive action in immigrant areas — even though the fact was disguised by describing them as 'urban areas of special need' (Edwards and Batley 1978, 46). It seems clear that the programme was not a considered policy, rather a hasty response to the political problem of the day. Yet the form of presentation reflects an equally important political perception: that only if aid were dispensed even-handedly as between immigrant and indigenous populations, would such a policy prove politically acceptable.

Urgent political concerns about immigration, to be fair, were only one element in the discovery of the inner city problem. Equally significant was the appearance, within a short period, of important reports which in different ways focused attention on it: the Milner Holland report of 1965 on London housing, the Plowden report of 1967 on primary schools, and the Seebohm report of 1968 on the coordination of social services for deprived individuals and families. This happened at the same time as 'rediscovery of poverty' by the school of Richard Titmuss at the London School of Economics, which challenged the comfortable belief that economic growth and marginally improved benefits would cure the problem of poverty (Abel-Smith and Townsend 1965). At the same time, small area data — available for the first time from the 1961 Census — made it possible to pinpoint the existence of local concentrations of deprivation. In the years 1965–8 these influences came together and united with the older tradition of physical planning improvement, to produce a new policy thrust that dominated the next decade.

The Evolution of Policy Initiatives

The first two of these inner city initiatives neatly illustrate these multiple influences. *Section 11 of the Local Government Act of 1966* provided that local authorities with substantial numbers of Commonwealth immigrants could receive 75 percent central government grants for approved expenditures in such fields as education, child care and maternity services. In practice more than 80 percent of expenditure went to education, the bulk of it to specialist teachers in language and remedial skills for children. An attempt to replace this provision by a more comprehensive measure was rejected on grounds of economy by the Conservative administration in 1980.

Following the 1966 Act, the *Educational Priority Area* (EPA) programmes of 1967–8 stemmed directly from the recommendations of
the Plowden report, but were undoubtedly also influenced by the
rejection by many local education authorities – including London and
Birmingham – of earlier government proposals to disperse non-white
students. Though only elements of the Plowden proposals were actually
implemented, the EPAs – with their special building programmes, their
special allowances to teachers in deprived areas, and their action research programmes – were the first specific area-based programmes
focused particularly on inner cities and similar deprived environments.
Further, they represented an innovation in that the schools qualifying
for special allowances were selected on the basis of specific social
indicators. But in one respect the policy was conventional: the notion
in the Plowden report that people in deprived areas were caught in a
'vicious circle' of deprivation that could be remedied by education,
accorded with the 'culture of poverty' theory then current (McKay and
Cox 1979a, 236).

The *Urban Programme*, a Home Office initiative, followed in 1968.
Put together in response to the Powell speech, and apparently owing
little or nothing to any other outside influence, it too stressed the
provision of aid to combat local pockets of deprivation, defined in
terms of social indicators – overcrowding, large families, unemployment, poor environment, immigrant concentrations, children in care or
in need of care – which were however never quantified. This aid was
provided on a 75:25 basis by central and local government. The Home
Office hoped that it would be used for programmes that local authorities otherwise could not – or would not – undertake. In practice,
much of the spending was on items that a good local authority might be
expected to provide anyway. In the first four years most of the money
went on day nurseries, nursery education and child care. But none of
the sums involved was very large.

However, after 1975 the Urban Programme was greatly expanded in
scale. Spending on it increased from £29.8 million in 1977 to no less
than £165.0 million in 1979/80. But this reflects the impact of the
Partnership and Programme area schemes, introduced after 1977, which
are described below. The so-called Traditional Urban Programme, which
is the pre-1977 programme, was still only accounting for £26.6 million
in 1979/80. By that time, though, the emphasis of the programme had
changed. Spending on provision for children, which had accounted for
nearly 53 percent of the total budget in the period 1968–73, was down
to 30 percent during 1978–80. By the latter date 20.4 percent of the

expenditure went to community projects, close on 13 percent to special education, and a similar percentage to other age groups. Thus the traditional programme was much more diversified than in its earlier years. In 1980 the Department of the Environment — which had taken over responsibility for the Urban Programme in 1975 — appraised its future. It resolved to retain the traditional programme at roughly its then present level, but with a greater emphasis on the involvement of community groups.

The *Community Development Projects* (CDPs) were another Home Office initiative, from 1969, which — like the Urban Programme — owed much to one official, Derek Morrell. This time there was a direct American influence in the emphasis on raising the people of deprived areas from what was seen as 'fatalistic dependence' on local council bureaucracies, to independence and self-sufficiency. The means to this end was the creation of twelve local teams, similar to those created in the United States under the 1964 Equal Opportunities Act, who were to work closely with local deprived communities, monitored by an action research team drawn usually from the local university or polytechnic. (An original feature of the plan — a central research and monitoring team inside the Home Office — never materialised.) Predictably, as in the United States, the teams soon ran into conflict not only with the more traditional, hierarchical local government bureaucracies but also with the local community — particularly since, perhaps frustrated by what they saw as obstacles in their path, many of them soon embraced Marxist explanations of the plight of the people of the deprived areas. In 1976, clearly attempting to maintain good relations with the local authorities, the Home Office dispersed the teams and abruptly terminated the experiment (McKay and Cox 1979a, 244–5).

The *Comprehensive Community Programmes* (CCPs), from 1974 onwards, were evidently designed to act as a more acceptable substitute for the CDPs. They were supposed to consist in the comprehensive analysis of the needs of deprived areas and of proposals for meeting them — again posited on the concept of area-based discrimination to grapple with the problem of deprivation. But it was never clear how the programmes could be comprehensive without the cooperation of other home policy departments who were responsible for most of the substantive policy areas involved. In fact, the initiative produced little more than pilot research projects in the three areas in question (McKay and Cox 1979a, 249–50).

A much more substantial initiative, with a clear outcome, came from

the Department of the Environment. The *Housing Action Areas*, introduced in the 1974 Housing Act, marked an important stage in the
conversion of the Department of the Environment to policies of urban
rehabilitation rather than urban renewal, as foreshadowed in the 1968
White Paper *Old Houses into New Homes* (Ministry of Housing and
Local Government 1968). They involved special levels of grant to
owner-occupiers and landlords for housing improvement in small,
defined areas of older housing, with the aim of upgrading the whole
area very substantially in a short period. The justification was clearly
that the areas would generate a 'demonstration effect', producing
quicker and better results than if the efforts were spread. Significantly,
unlike the Home Office initiatives, the HAAs were thus justified prag-
matically, and not on the basis of a particular concept of deprivation.
Yet, as before, they were specifically area-based policies.

A Turning Point

The most important turning point came in a further initiative from the
Department of the Environment: the *Inner Area Studies* carried out by
consultants between 1972 and 1977. What was most interesting about
them was their ambivalent character. Like previous exercises, they were
area-based and even small-area-based: the 'inner areas' under study
ranged in population from about 40,000 to 60,000. But unlike all
previous experiments, they were deliberately set up to take a 'total
approach' to an understanding of the problem (McKay and Cox 1979a,
246–7). In practice, the consultants were inevitably influenced by two
main streams of thinking in the mid-1970s: first, a 'liberal' line that
sought the reasons for economic decline; secondly, a related Marxist
line – derived from the conclusions of the CDP studies, then being
published – that emphasised the same theme but preferred explanations in terms of the investment strategies of large capitalist
corporations.

The resulting thrust of the consultants' reports (Department of the
Environment 1977a) and of the White Paper *Policy for the Inner Cities*
(DoE 1977b) that emerged from it, was therefore to give more
emphasis to the economic problems of the cities and to possible ways
of meeting them. This represented a major change, for when the consultants were commissioned the main emphasis had been far more on
the Department's traditional concern with the physical environment.
Indeed, from one aspect the whole initiative can be epitomised as an
attempt on the part of DoE to wrest control of inner city programmes
not merely from the Home Office – whose responsibilities had been

derived somewhat ambiguously from its concern with problems of social malaise — but also from the Department of Industry, the traditional guardians of regional policy. As already noted, in 1975 the Urban Programme was transferred to the DoE.

At any event, the 1977 White Paper — and the 1978 Inner Urban Areas Act that followed it — represented the biggest single policy shift since inner urban policies were introduced. Though area-based positive discrimination measures with a primarily social service orientation continued, the new emphasis was strongly on 'economic revival'. Henceforth inner cities would have first place, after Assisted Areas (with which in part they coincided), in the grant of industrial development certificates, and would thus take precedence over the new towns. Existing programmes were to be coordinated to aid inner areas. The rate support grant formula was to be adjusted so as to give even more help to inner urban areas. Finally, the urban programme was to be greatly expanded, and Central/Local Government Partnerships were to be introduced for some of the biggest cities, together with smaller programmes of specific aid for other cities. In parallel, Glasgow would get extra aid — especially for its Glasgow Eastern Area Renewal Programme (GEAR).

How far, in practice, there really was a shift is debatable. In the first place, as some critics pointed out, the extra resources in the urban programme were really marginal compared with the total amount of local authority spending in these deprived areas. In Liverpool it was officially estimated that they added 5 percent to total local authority income, not a negligible figure but not a major addition either. Still, they were uncommitted resources and they did coincide, in the late 1970s, with shifts in rate support grant and with internal shifts in local authority spending, which probably favoured their inner urban areas. In this light, the revamping of the rate support grant — itself later reversed by the subsequent Conservative Government — was probably much more significant, since it affected the scale of the so-called main programmes. Secondly, the partnerships seem to have gone in very different directions. Especially in the first year, they tended to take down projects and programmes that were gathering dust on bureaucratic shelves, and these reflected the traditional interests of local authority spending departments rather than represented any bold new initiative. So, instead of major programmes to encourage economic revival, in some partnerships some of the authorities tended to spend the extra funds on parks and swimming pools and community groups. There was a disproportionate stress on capital projects, and little sense of planning by objective (Hall 1978, 618; Nabarro and McDonald 1978, 172; Stewart and Underwood 1980, 5).

Tory Initiatives

The Conservative approach to the inner city problem, since the May 1979 election, has been to continue with the partnership initiative — though with the important proviso that rate support grant to the cities is to be reduced, and cash limits on local authority spending — earlier introduced by the previous Labour administration — would be stringently enforced. This is clearly shifting the Partnerships and Programmes in directions away from social programmes and towards wealth-generating activities (Stewart and Underwood 1980, 7). But in addition, there are two quite new initiatives. In the first place, two largely derelict areas — the London and Liverpool docklands — have been placed under the direction of *Urban Development Corporations* (UDCs), which in many ways follow the model of the New Town Development Corporations in having considerable day-to-day commercial freedom. They take over many of the traditional functions of local government in their areas. The argument for such a solution, despite its undemocratic character, is that ordinary local authorities would find such a large-scale development task beyond their capacities, especially if — as in London — responsibility is shared between the Greater London Council and several boroughs. Almost unprecedently in the history of inner city policies, this met with attack from the Labour Party — perhaps unsurprisingly, since many of the local authorities to be displaced were Labour ones.

The other initiative has however proved even more controversial. *Enterprise Zones*, announced by the Chancellor of the Exchequer in his 1980 Budget speech, are to be areas — again the most derelict parts of the inner cities and elsewhere — where most forms of planning and control are to be lifted. In practice they will have greatly simplified planning regulations, plus freedom from local rates and other tax concessions, plus removal of other kinds of regulations (such as the requirement to file statistical returns and contribute to training board levies). They have been bitterly attacked by the National Executive of the Labour Party on the ground that they will introduce Hong Kong-style sweated industry into Britain, and will do little save attract mobile economic activities from other depressed inner city areas. Together, then, these two measures seem to mark the breakdown of a decade of bi-partisan consensus over inner city policy. But this probably reflects the sharply changed perception of what constitutes the inner city problem, and the associated sharp cleavage of opinion on how to solve it, in an era of recession. In any event, local Labour councils have broken with the National Executive of the party over the Enterprise Zone issue, sometimes positively scrambling for the extra aid that is involved.

The Initiatives Analysed

It can thus be seen that broadly, from 1967 to 1974 — when the DoE's inner city consultants insisted on a radical recasting of their briefs — there was a certain continuity and similarity in the inner city policy-initiatives. Then, suddenly, there was a sharp break and a new set of emphases. In what follows we try to draw out some of the common themes, with special attention to the period down to 1977, and with reference to the nature of the change that then received official sanction in the White Paper on inner city policy. We look first at the underlying philosophy — or, as some would say, ideology — behind the policies, at the objectives, and finally at the methods (with particular reference to the selection of areas and the criteria employed for this purpose) and the action research that accompanied many of the pro-grammes. In the next section we consider the somewhat complex central-local government relationships that developed as a result of these initiatives.

Early preconceptions

As already seen, the early Educational Priority Areas programme and much of the subsequent Urban Aid programme were dominated by the notion of individual or social inadequacies and of the 'cycle of depriva-tion' — hence their emphasis on family support services, pre-school programmes and family planning. This approach reached its peak in the Transmitted Deprivation studies which were launched after Sir Keith Joseph's initiative of 1972. Even in the area management studies, there was an implicit belief that improved service delivery would 'reduce intrinsically anti-social family pathologies or inadequacies' (Lawless 1979, 146). The belief that deprivation was an essentially residual phenomenon justified the essentially supplementary character of the 'associated programmes'. The economic and social machinery was regarded as working well, save for a minority of families who tended to misuse it. Positive discrimination would solve these problems, through what Wick described as the 'common attempt by government to distribute resources more specifically and, by implication, more effectively and more economically' (Wick 1977, 51). But this formulation departed from the original formulation of positive discrimination by Titmuss, which implied a more fundamental redistribution.

Revised ideas

The original conception saw the role of inner city policy as a special and limited one, dealing with individual problem families within a generally prosperous economy. But already, by the late 1960s and early 1970s, it was possible to recognise that the inner cities represented a special problem (Donnison and Eversley 1973, Eversley 1973). Writers like Donnison, Eversley, Evans and Lomas relentlessly pursued this argument, and effectively from 1972 onward — when the Department of the Environment appointed the three inner urban area consultants — the point was accepted officially. Thus, while the Community Development Project teams claimed much of the credit for this, they were far from alone in it. Though they had been appointed on the basis of an underlying assumption that problems of urban deprivation had their origin in the individual pathologies of local populations, they soon rejected this view. Instead, they sought explanations of urban decay in 'the changing economic bases within an era of national and international slump' (Lawless 1979, 215). Thus they came to see poverty as engendered by the competition for resources under the capitalist system, which also helped preserve the existing divisions of society and thereby the unequal distribution resources.

Consensus on structural causes

Although the Marxist view was rejected by many urban observers, they shared with the Marxists a recognition that local individuals and communities depended upon changes made at national or international level. Thus the Liverpool Inner Area Study team admitted that they had 'moved from our original statement of local issues which gave rise to the action projects to one which raised issues of fundamental importance to people's opportunities for housing and a job' (Department of the Environment 1977c). The Inner Area Teams specifically rejected an approach that ascribed the plight of the inner cities to the crisis of capitalism — though they did stress that it did depend on deep economic causes and that its treatment would therefore depend on a total approach that tackled these causes. In other words, they were structuralists in the strict sense that they ascribed the inner cities' problems to deep structural causes (albeit with important local variations) — but they were not structuralists in the common usage, which means Marxist. The difference was simply that the non-Marxists believed that the system was capable of adaptation and response; the Marxists believed that it was not, and was doomed to destruction. It would certainly be going too far to claim that the resulting policies — both the partnership schemes and the general pattern of fiscal redistribution — match up to the conclusions of this analysis, yet the programmes initiated by the 1974-9 Labour Government certainly reveal an awareness that the basic problems are of more general origin and consequence than seemed acceptable when the first Urban Programme was designed in the late 1960s.

The policies of the 1979 Conservative Government, too, reflect acceptance of the thesis that inner urban areas are now faced with major economic decline requiring a radical break with previous policies. True, it seems likely that the Urban Development Corporations and the Enterprise Zones — like the partnerships which they supplement — will in practice make only a marginal difference to the general downward trend, though they will doubtless have a considerable impact in the areas where they are established. But, from a theoretical standpoint, it is the changed recognition of reality that is important. As McKay and Cox point out, it essentially took the policy-makers a decade to appreciate that they were facing a problem of structural urban decline (McKay and Cox 1979a, 251-3). This is in itself odd, since urban researchers — of both the Marxist and non-Marxist variety — had been stressing the fact since about 1970. But not until the reports of the Inner Area teams did this new view receive unreserved official acceptance.

In retrospect, as McKay and Cox conclude, the whole policy of the 1967-77 period was based on a very strange perception of the problem to be handled. Neither political-party debate, nor professional discussion in planning circles, had much influence. Accordingly, the whole policy was implemented in almost total isolation from the mainstream policies in housing, land use planning and transport. The central notion — of pockets of 'multiple deprivation' experienced by individuals in small pockets of urban decline — seems to have been generated by some civil servants and politicians within the Home Office, and influenced by some then fashionable ideas but not supported by factual evidence — which, when it eventually emerged, contradicted the whole notion (McKay and Cox 1979a, 248).

The conclusion is that during the period down to 1977, an intuitive-intellectual perception of a problem (multiple deprivation in small areas) became allied with a political initiative deriving partly — though not totally — from a perceived need to provide answers to racial concentrations in some inner cities. The shift after 1977 seems to have had similar origins. A different intellectual paradigm — of structural decline — became allied to similar political concerns, including continued concern about racial problems (and particularly about minority unemployment), and a worry on the part of Labour politicians that depopulation was changing the electoral balance in the cities (McKay and Cox 1979, 255-6). The critical difference is that after 1977 the prevailing theory had better empirical backing.

Objectives

Many commentators have pointed out that the aims of the various urban programmes were never clearly formulated. Edwards and Batley, for example, assert that no specific research brief was provided by the Home Office for the urban programmes. Certainly those involved in both the Community Development Projects and the Inner Area Studies were able, to a greater or lesser extent, to adapt their terms of reference to suit their own perceptions of the immediate needs. In the case of the Community Development Projects, it was in part the changes in national and local political administrations in 1969 and 1970 that created the political space within which those engaged in the projects were able to innovate — at least initially, since before long the new Conservative administrations both in Whitehall and in town halls developed suspicions about the programme. Another contributory factor was the speed with which policies like the Urban Programme were introduced.

Nonetheless, it is possible to discern three dominant themes which run through the various policies initiated during this period. One is the coordination of the planning and delivery of urban public services. This stands out clearly in the Educational Priority Areas, which were interested in promoting coordination between home and school: in the original objectives of the Community Development Projects — and of the Comprehensive Community Programmes that succeeded them; in the 'total approach' of the Inner Area Studies; and finally in the stress of the 1977 White Paper on a more 'unified' approach to urban problems. A second objective was the development of area management as the decentralised corollary of corporate management schemes in local government generally. This was made explicitly in the terms of reference of the Inner Area Studies. It followed the recommendations of the Bains Committee on local authority administration (Department of the Environment 1972).

The third theme that runs through the various inner city initiatives is the need to encourage public participation. This too flowed from the conclusions of a previous policy review, in this case the work of the Skeffington Committee (Ministry of Housing and Local Government 1969). Participation was seen as the opposite side of the coin of responsive local administration. There was therefore a close parallel between the general objective of, for example, the Community Development Projects and the preceeding developments in planning thinking. Subsequently, the Quality of Life Studies, the Urban Guidelines project, the Inner Area Studies and the Inner City policy White Paper all stressed the importance of participation. The common element between each of these objectives is the focus on local government and institutional processes. This demonstrates one of the strongest biases in the development of inner city policy in this country and differentiates it clearly from the American example with its much greater reliance on voluntary and grass-roots organisations.

Selection of Areas

As already seen, the initiatives of the 1967-77 period shared a general consensus that the inner city problem consisted in multiple deprivation among small residual groups in small inner city areas, some of which areas would receive intensive remedial treatment to see whether this might also work for all the others. But, because of the relative paucity of empirical work on the very phenomenon, in practice there was much variation between studies and within programmes on the question of the most appropriate and reliable social indicators with which to measure deprivation.

The Urban Programme and the Educational Priority Areas social indicators reflected the 'cycle of deprivation' theory. The former included delinquents, large families, alcoholics and the mentally ill in one of the circulars setting out its social indicators. The Plowden Committee similarly suggested that the following indicators should be used to designate Educational Priority Areas: occupation of heads of households; size of family; overcrowding and sharing; benefits' claimants; poor attendance and truancy; the percentage of retarded, disturbed and handicapped children; incomplete families; pupils unable to speak English.

It was characteristic of the Urban Programme and most of the other urban deprivation programmes, however, that the criteria were somewhat elusive. In some cases they changed during the course of a programme or else they were never very clearly stated. This allowed administrators to respond flexibly to pressures to include a wider range of projects and areas, and it was probably easier to handle politically. Standardised criteria were thus not encouraged and there was much variation in the indices adopted between local authorities involved in the urban programmes. When attempts were made to quantify the criteria, they relied heavily on census data and this tended both to blur the distinction between causes and symptoms and to introduce a physical bias, because of the large number of items relating to housing. After 1975, increasing attention was paid to economic criteria such as the loss of employment in manufacturing, unemployment, low levels of investments and wage rates.

In practice, however, the choice of priority areas left considerable scope for self-selection by the local authorities concerned. Certainly some local authorities rejected offers to participate in such schemes as the Educational Priority Areas programme and the Community Development Projects. Objective criteria have tended to yield place to political leverage, with the result that the same cities have tended to participate in each successive new initiative.

A very similar story seems to emerge from the selection of the Partnership areas in 1977 and the Enterprise Zones in 1980. In both, the decisions were taken extremely quickly after announcement of the general features of the scheme. In both, it seems that a crucial feature was the need to spread the schemes fairly evenly across the country for political reasons, especially as between London and the Assisted Areas, regardless of the precise scale of the need or the suitability of the area for such treatment. In no case does it appear that an extended analysis was made. The tradition of 'ad hockery' in British governmental decision-making, it appears, dies hard.

The role of research

One important and innovative aspect of the new inner city policies was the role given to research — and, especially in the early initiatives, action research. This was pioneered by the Educational Priority Areas team and described by Halsey as 'small-scale interventions in the functioning of the real world, usually in administrative systems, and the close examination of the effects of such intervention' (Department of Education and Science 1972, 165). The Inner Area Studies recognised the importance of linking research to action, the Birmingham team including among its revised objectives the intention 'To investigate by experimental action methods of improving the environment of inner areas' (Department of the Environment 1977d, 2). Many of the other programmes were also influenced by this approach.

In practice it created many problems. Monitoring was typically undertaken by a local action team working in conjunction with a research unit based in a local institution or local government department. As the Community Development Project teams found, this relationship was far from easy. While the action teams resented what they saw as the research teams' lack of a direct contribution to overcoming deprivation, the latter felt that the action teams misunderstood the role of research (Lawless 1979, 124-6). Another problem was that individual action project findings were not always integrated sufficiently into a wider framework to be able to test general hypotheses. As Edwards and Batley (1978) point out, the Urban Programme signally failed to achieve a monitoring system capable of feeding back to the various project teams. The official reasons given were staff shortages and hesitation over selecting information suitable and relevant for other projects, but this is clearly less than the whole story. As Lawless (1979, 87) comments, 'the pitfalls of action research as a methodological process were evidently understood, partly because of an appreciation of the experience of this approach in other urban initiatives'.

Central-local-voluntary group relations

The conduct of the various inner city programmes, and in particular of the research that accompanied them, was strongly influenced by their relationship with government. Almost certainly the approach both to action and to research would have been very different if, as for example in the United States, much greater direct responsibility had been devolved to voluntary organisations. Of all the programmes considered, the Community Development Projects probably achieved the greatest effective freedom from governmental control. But the struggle to achieve this independence of view and of action clearly affected the stance adopted by the more radical project teams.

All the urban deprivation programmes were sponsored by a major central government department. The Home Office took many of the early initiatives: the Urban Programme, the CDPs, and the CCPs. However — following an unproductive rivalry and duplication of efforts between the two departments — the Department of the Environment took over the leading role, with responsibility for the Inner Area Studies (in 1972) and the central/local government partnerships together with the Urban Programme (in 1977). In the case of the Urban

Programme other departments — Environment, Health and Social Security — were involved under Home Office aegis. The Inner Area Studies and the Partnerships had a minister chairing their steering committees. This central government involvement somewhat reduced the autonomy of the local authority, though it did increase the prospect of influencing policy.

However, in many cases the local authority also played a crucial role, which invariably took the form of several local authority representatives with seats on the steering committee. Voluntary organisations might be involved too — a fact that sometimes produced tensions between them and the local authorities, as in the Urban Programme and especially the CDPs (Higgens 1979, 79). In the case of the CDPs, this led to much wasted effort in attacking the local authorities in a provocative and inept way — almost as if to prove that the local council was an agent of social control. But in extenuation, it must be said that the teams were given a structurally impossible remit and an almost impossible political climate in which to work. Yet, in most of the other area-based projects, relationships were less strained. In the case of the Inner Area Studies this was almost certainly true because — perhaps learning from the CDP experience — the Department of the Environment employed professional private consultants to undertake the research. Further, though these consultants tried to take an independent position, it is probably true that they say their first relationship was with the local authority rather than with those who might have been regarded as the representatives of the community.

The main basis of the central-local relationship on the area-based programmes was of course a financial one. The Urban Programme helped — among other schemes — to finance the EPAs and the CDPs, leaving the local authorities to pay only the remaining 25 percent, and this was eligible for rate support grant, so the actual cost to the local authority was far less (Lansley 1979, 56-63). Similar arrangements applied to other schemes. The central government funded the Inner Area Studies in their entirety. In some cases, central government's share might be limited to a particular category of spending. In the case of the CCPs, for instance, it covered only staff costs.

It seems clear that by 1975 the Urban Programme — then amounting to some £16.6 million a year — had become the central government's chief instrument for diverting resources to disadvantaged areas. By this time it was being drawn from the rate support grant — instead of being supplemental to it, as in the early years — and it could be regarded therefore as some kind of redistributive mechanism. But down to this time it was somewhat marginal (Kennett 1980b, 56).

Overall, specific grants like the Urban Programme grew rapidly after 1977, but are still a small part of total central government support to local authorities. Thus in 1979/80 the Urban Programme amounted to £165 million, the great majority of which went to Partnership and Programme areas. Far more important in total is rate support grant (£7 258 million in 1979/80), which accounts for no less than 87 percent of the Aggregate Exchequer Grant (Kennett 1980b, 73). Though no formal statement is available of the precise objectives of the RSG system, it is clear that as well as making a general contribution to local authority expenditure in recognition of the role that local government plays in fulfilling central government policies, the system has three main objectives: to compensate for lack of local resources, to provide extra resources to meet extra needs, and to relieve the burden of rate increases on domestic ratepayers. Each of these three aims was, until 1981, met by a specific element in RSG.

Developing an analogy of Foster (Foster 1977) one can say that the RSG used until 1981 resembled a philanthropist giving aid. He first decides that he will help only members of a certain family (the domestic element); then he gives a first set of presents, levelling the poorest up till they have a standard minimum (the resources element); then he donates a second sum depending on the family size or the condition of their homes (the needs element). After 1974 the resources element was increased to nearly one third of the total amount, and the formula for calculating it was altered so that it was focused more sharply on areas with severe social problems. But it is still a blunt instrument: most authorities attract it, and the more revenue any one local authority raises, the more resources grant it attracts. Further — and perversely — an authority with a declining population finds itself with more rateable value per head and this in turn may reduce its resources element; while if it is then successful in attracting new industrial or commercial rateable value, it then loses resources element pound for pound.

The needs element is more than twice the resources element, and its potential capacity for achieving social justice is evidently greater. But for this purpose, again, it is a very blunt weapon. It tends to be based on past expenditure, so that a well-off authority with high spending on (say) education simply attracts more grant. There is no allowance for quality of service provided, or for cost-of-living variations between authorities (Kennett 1980b, 38-40). After 1974 the formula was altered to the benefit of metropolitan districts and above all the London boroughs. But the aid did not pass to the poorest boroughs. Haringey,

Ealing, Havering and Newham — all boroughs with areas of stress — lost grant income in 1979, while Westminster and Kensington/Chelsea gained (Kennett 1980b, 48). Inequitable as this may have seemed, the arbitrary formula that replaced it in 1981 promises to be much more so.

Perhaps the strangest feature of the central-local relationship in most of these schemes was how far it seemed to exist in a hermetically sealed compartment. For all the talk about the 'corporate planning' or the 'total approach' the initiatives do not seem to have been related very clearly to what was happening in all the other areas of government policy. The nearest approach to a major policy review was undoubtedly the 1977 White Paper, with its changes in industrial location policy and its shift in rate support grant. But, while the partnerships were set up specifically to allocate the additional resources thus released, in practice the shift was extremely marginal. To a large degree the existing government programmes rolled on as before — and there was no hint, as there was in the approach then being developed by the Department of Housing and Urban Development in the United States, of urban impact analysis to evaluate the total effect on urban areas of government spending programmes across the board.

Waiting for a Verdict

To reach a verdict on this large and varied bundle of programmes is no easy task. For one thing, some of the most important are still in progress, and therefore almost impossible to evaluate in any definitive way. For another, those that have largely or completely finished — the first wave of 1967–72 — often tended to have very vaguely defined aims, so it is difficult to say how far they achieved them. The most that can reasonably be done is to make some interim assessment as a contribution to a debate that is still continuing as we conclude. We ask, first, how the programmes have affected policy-makers' understanding of the problem; second, how they have generally affected the evolution of social policy.

How effective?

The Section 11 provisions and the *Educational Priority Areas*, first in chronological sequence, initiated additional teaching aid in areas of immigrant concentration, introduced differentially higher teachers' pay in the designated area, provided more teachers' aids and increased capital expenditure as well as extending provision for nursery education.

The *Urban Programme* has had a longer and more varied history. Its funds have been used for a variety of purposes, with a special emphasis on filling gaps in spending departments' programmes. Much of the money has gone on social provision, related especially to pre-school education in the late 1960s and early 1970s, later to recreation and community facilities and — after 1977 — to employment. But the funds have never been large in comparison with total local authority budgets. Latterly the great bulk of the expanded programme has gone to Partnership and Programme authorities, leaving only £27 million out of £165 million (in 1979—80) for the so-called Traditional Urban Programme. The funds have been very concentrated: 17 out of 89 eligible authorities got half the funds in 1978—9, and it seems likely that if the aim was to help deprived people and groups the money might often have been better spent in other ways.

The *Community Development Projects*, overall achieved limited results in terms of action — though one should not neglect the role they played in encouraging local residents to control and operate services such as law and information centres, as in Hillfields, Coventry or Batley. They also played a more general role in policy formulation, through the evidence they gave to the Allen Committee on rates, or the Layfield Committee on local government finance. In any event, perhaps they were never expected to achieve spectacular practical results. Their fundamental contribution was not there but in conceptual thinking. They showed that deprived areas were not just concentrated in the conurbations, but covered a wide spectrum of places from Oldham or North Tyneside to Cleator Moor in Cumbria, a deprived small town in a rural area. They thus helped to refute the prevailing notion that deprivation was merely a matter of small pockets in inner urban areas — though in this work, as already seen, they were certainly not alone. And they helped to shift the dominant paradigm away from poverty as seen in terms of individual misfortune or inadequacy, to poverty as a result of powerful structural forces outside the individual's control. Here again, though, they were certainly not the only voices making this point.

The *Quality of Life* studies spent a generous budget of £1 million — more than most other initiatives — chiefly to promote leisure activities. The scheme did not concern itself specifically with problems of urban deprivation at all. Lawless, perhaps over stating the case, concludes that it had 'strong claims to the most irrelevant initiative ever devised by central government in its long search to eradicate urban deprivation on the cheap' (Lawless 1979, 88). But, perhaps to make amends, the

Department of the Environment did subsequently commission a study of recreation and deprivation in inner urban areas, which concentrated on provision for deprived groups (DoE 1977e). The Urban Guidelines, launched by the Department of the Environment at the same time as the Inner Area Studies, were three studies by consultants, in three separate towns, supposed to see whether it was possible to devise a 'total approach' — in other words, a corporate approach — to urban problems. The results varied in quality: one, for Sunderland, was thought reasonably successful; another, for Rotherham, did not win much support.

Of all the initiatives, the *Inner Area Studies* seem to have been thought by most commentators to have been the most influential in terms of subsequent policy. They had quite considerable publicity on publication in 1967. They were little read, but probably did change ministers' perceptions of the problem. The resulting White Paper identified its debt to the studies, by emphasising the need for a coordinated approach to inner city problems; by shifting the emphasis in Industrial Development Certificate policy towards the inner areas; by shifting financial resources generally in the same direction through the changes in RSG formula; and through the Partnership and Programme schemes. These last schemes are themselves still evolving, and it seems premature to evaluate them. In the early years they did suffer from an emphasis on schemes already prepared, many with a social or recreational aspect rather than a specific aim of economic regeneration. But, as the initiatives have gathered pace and as local authorities have recognised their new role in attracting and developing employment, they may have come rather closer to their original objectives.

Consistent emphasis

Overall, throughout the history of the initiatives — from Educational Priority Areas to Enterprise Zones — one can see the same consistent emphasis on area-based policies. The reasons for this are complex. Some commentators suggest that the popularity of such programmes is that they combine low cost and high visibility. But that may be too cynical. However, the sums involved have tended to be small — though lately they have risen sharply. The Urban Programme received considerable publicity at its inception, yet by 1976 it was accounting for ¼ percent of the RSG (Townsend 1976, 169). Between then and 1979 it increased from £30 million to £165 million, but is still a very small fraction of RSG — albeit heavily concentrated.

Coupled with this was a reluctance on the part of many politicians —

Labour as well as Conservative — to agree to constant rises in social service spending and in the proportion of people dependent on the welfare state. This trend, Richard Crossman pointed out, could soon meet resistance not only from the middle class but also from working class taxpayers who would have to foot the bill (Kincaid 1973, 11). Selectivity, not universality, was therefore the order of the day and area policies were a crude and easy way of achieving selectivity — or so it was thought. There was another good reason for area-based policies, especially in periods of expenditure restraint: the support they won from advocates of better coordination and corporate management, who saw the possibility of organisational reform that would deliver better services at no greater (or even lower) cost. Deprived urban areas will tend to appear as ideal laboratories for such experiments — hence the Urban Guidelines and Area Management schemes.

Yet another justification, appealing perhaps to a rather different constituency of politicians and officials, lies in a worry about the increasing size and remoteness of government from the citizens. Area-based policies, it is suggested, give an opportunity for 'the governmental system to learn about and respond to people's needs as they themselves define them' (Hambleton 1977, 15). It is thus a positive step towards extending democracy. But the CDP teams had an alternative, less charitable explanation: the aim, as they saw it, was to allow the state to keep its finger on the working-class pulse as a surveillance device and in order to be able to prepare the next piece of ameliorative action (Community Development Project 1977, 57).

Limited success

Whether one shares the conspiratorial view of politics or not, there are good reasons for concluding that overall, the whole bundle of policies has aroused a great deal of activity, has spent modest, though increasing amounts of money, and has achieved modest results in measurable terms so far. The critical question must be how far the inner city areas, or, indeed any other areas of Britain, have been changed by the initiatives. To that, the most realistic answer to that must be, very little up to now, though the picture may change. Projects or no projects, resources could certainly have been targeted to deprived areas and deprived groups by means of the traditional rate support grant mechanism. Slum clearance and rehabilitation, replanning, clearance of derelict land, rebuilding of schools, the improvement of urban transport would have all continued — as indeed they did, virtually unaffected by the initiatives. In the context of the entire range of public policies and the overall programme of public spending at central and local government levels, some of the initiatives amounted to little more than minor gimmicks. Others had an impact in their defined areas, albeit marginally. The Partnerships and Programmes, and the Enterprise Zones and Urban Development Corporations that followed them, promise a bigger impact.

That is even more true when we consider some of the thrusts and impacts of these other programmes in closely related areas. In housing, the bi-partisan policy of massive income support to owner-occupied housing helped accelerate the flight of middle-class and skilled working-class families from the inner cities. So did the New Towns Programme, marginally cut back — but certainly not stopped in its tracks — as a result of the 1977 White Paper. In transport, the roads programme significantly improved transport between and around the cities while doing relatively little, in comparison, for the most congested and the most depressed inner urban industrial areas. Similarly, the policy throughout most of the postwar period — of restricted subsidy for public transport — has had a clear impact on the declining levels of access for poorer people in inner city areas. In education, the comprehensive school revolution has tended to produce neighbourhood schools in which deprived neighbourhood children are gathered together with other deprived inner city children to receive an education which — despite additional resources — is often significantly poorer than received by their suburban or rural counterparts. In health, the reallocation of resources is tending to the advantage of the still growing suburbs and exurbs, at the expense of the problems of old hospitals and inadequate general practitioner facilities in the older urban areas.

By and large, therefore, most of the specific inner city policy initiatives were little more than minor and peripheral experiments. They did not attempt much and they did not achieve much, however much they may have been oversold by politicians anxious to prove their *bona fides* to the electorate. Ironically, the main gain was in understanding that the problem has much deeper roots than we imagined before — but armed with the understanding we can see just how much more difficult it is to do anything about it. This is a harsh verdict, and it applies particularly to the initiatives before the breakpoint of 1977. The initiatives since then — the Partnerships, the Programmes, the extended Urban Programme, the Urban Development Corporation — are of a different order. They promise much more, and they may yet — despite all difficulties — deliver. But a verdict is somewhat premature.

Some Unanswered Questions

The main question that still lies massively open concerns the roots of urban change. Since the mid-1970s, we have seen, policy makers have come to appreciate that the problem of the inner cities must be tackled at its source, in terms of the diminishing economic base and the inability of the local community to create new sources of innovative activity, coupled with the increasing unattractiveness of such areas to outside capital. That appreciation lies at the heart of the Partnership and Programme initiatives, which are still fundamentally at the experimental stage. Still lacking is any real appreciation of the precise combination of forces that causes individual cities or regions to grow or to decline. That, as already indicated in the conclusions to Chapter 2, must figure first on any future research agenda.

Equally important, however, is to understand how far the whole bundle of government policies — not just so-called inner city policies, but policies in all kinds of related areas, such as education, health, social security, housing and transport — have helped or hindered the cause of inner city regeneration. Already, at the close of Chapter 5, we have argued for the application in Britain of the American development of urban impact analysis. We merely underline that here. But associatedly, we believe that there is a need for better understanding of the basis of local authority finance in relation to needs and resources — both in terms of the pattern of central government aid, and in terms of the internal decision-making and allocating processes of local governments. We return to these points in the final chapter.

7 Retrospect and Prospect

Peter Hall

Cynics — or realists — might by now say that we have been here before and will doubtless be here again. The inner city problem, they may argue, is like the problem of the poor: it is always with us. For the poor, if one accepts the concept of relative deprivation, the old adage is by definition true. For the inner city, however, it is not necessarily true at all. In the first place, previous chapters have indicated that the so-called inner city problem may in fact be a series of separate problems that are not necessarily or directly related. There is a problem of structural industrial decline and a problem of concentrated deprivation, but the relationship between these is a subtle one that requires some teasing out. Secondly, we should by no means assume that geographical values remain unchanged. Once Liverpool and Glasgow boomed while Bristol languished; now the roles are reversed, while the rural areas of south east England — early in the twentieth century the scene of abject rural depression — are now among the most prosperous places in the country.

In this chapter, therefore, we look very briefly backward, and — at greater length, but with less certainty — forward. We ask whether the inner city in the past was seen as a problem for public policy, and if so what kind of problem. We ask what kinds of forces — technological, economic, social or cultural — could affect the future role of the inner cities in the life of Britain. We speculate on the kinds of problem that may loom uppermost for public policy in the year 2000, and on the question of whether such problems may be concentrated in particular areas or places — especially the inner cities.

The Inner City in History[1]

To find parallels and contrasts, we can usefully go back a century. The second half of the nineteenth century, and perhaps above all the 1880s,

[1] This section draws on Hebbert (1980), *The Inner City in Context*, Paper 5.

were distinguished by almost obsessive concern with the inner city, above all on the part of the media. H.M. Hyndman of the Social Democratic Foundation could complain at that time of a 'boom in slumming' (Hebbert 1980, 17). But the parallel lies not merely in the extreme visibility of the problem, but also in the explanations that contemporary observers found for it. One, the simplest, was that 'darkness and poverty were caused by sin' (Hebbert 1980, 20). The remedy, it was believed, was to be found in the settlement movement, which would communicate middle-class norms and modes of behaviour to the slum dweller. Re-interpret these aims in terms of the values and language of the 1960s, and we find more teachers, more nursery schools, more social workers — precisely the objectives of the urban deprivation programmes of that time.

A second explanation was more distinctively Victorian: that the physical surroundings of home and workplace were responsible for both the physical and the moral health of the workman. Starting with the basic notion of 'applications of lime and whitewash to houses and carbolic soap to their inhabitants' (Hebbert 1980, 22), this approach soon spread to a call for more and better housing, culminating in the first local authority housing programmes of the 1890s and in Ebenezer Howard's clarion call, in 1898, to disperse the urban slum dwellers. The parallel in the 1960s and 1970s, in the form of mass clearance and reconstruction of the Victorian urban fabric, can be seen as a long-delayed completion of that movement.

For the Victorians, there was yet a third explanation, which came to the fore in the 1880s: the plight of the urban poor arose simply from their poverty. Proof came in the classic surveys of Booth and Rowntree, which showed that the slum family simply could not afford the rent for a decent dwelling. Faced with the evidence, the Victorian social conscience showed a split: some continued to believe determinedly in the virtues of self-help, while others — including Booth's lieutenant, Beatrice Webb — came to hold that only a collectivist solution would provide an answer. The political spectrum has shifted in one hundred years: the significant split today is between Fabian advocates of radical income redistribution, and Marxist prophets of the collapse of the system, who were even to be found in the political debates of the 1880s. In the intervening time, it seems, neither analysis nor prescription have shown a really violent shift.

There is however one crucial difference. It is that the Victorian city was still a buoyant and growing city. People flooded in to seek their fortunes or at least to win a better living than they could find in the countryside. That was true whether they were Irish peasants pouring into Liverpool and Manchester after the potato failure of the 1840s, Essex farm labourers coming into East London in the wake of the agricultural depression of the 1870s, or Russian Jews from the small towns in the impoverished countryside of eastern Poland arriving en masse in east London in the 1890s. Conditions in the cities might seem wretched beyond description to us, but to the incomers they at least offered the hope of improvement. That was because, even more fundamentally, the Victorian city was still an economically dynamic place. New industries, or new versions of old industries, were being created all the time: ready-made clothing in London, bicycles and, later, cars in Birmingham, ships in Glasgow. Britain was the workshop of the world, and this was an urban workshop. In the last resort, it was because British entrepreneurs were still highly innovative and their industries were highly competitive. In truth, by the 1890s the writing was already on the wall: the Germans and the Americans were seizing the lead in innovation and in productive organisation (Allen 1976, 30-50). But the full consequences were not perceived for a long time. Indeed, as we have tried to show, it was only in the 1970s that researchers revealed the true extent of the collapse of the British urban economy.

The result is that the British inner city is no longer an attractive force. It was once overcrowded, poor and wretched, but it offered a step up the ladder of opportunity for millions of people. Thus, appalling a place as it might seem by the standards of the late twentieth century, it was — in the words and by the criteria of David Donnison — a Good City. Now it is generally not overcrowded (though pockets of it may be), less poor (though again there may be pockets of deprivation) and certainly less wretched. The critical point is that — with the exception of a small trickle of immigrants from the Indian subcontinent — it no longer seems a magnet; rather, those with the energy or the ability try to escape from it. It does not offer opportunities for its people or good life chances for their children. This is because it has somehow lost the mainspring of successful innovation and of economic creativity. It is, by the touchstones that matter, no longer the Good City.

That loss of spirit applies as much to the crucial decisions of the city fathers as to the thousands of smaller actions by individual entrepreneurs. Civically too, the feeling of enterprise seems to be slipping away. The Metropolitan Board of Works, in late Victorian London, swept away whole tracts of slum housing in order to create a totally new network of streets in the West End. To their energy and ruthlessness we owe Shaftesbury Avenue, Charing Cross Road, and Roseberry

Avenue. In contrast the Greater London Council — brought into being principally to provide an effective transportation plan for London — has dithered and changed course perpetually for a decade and a half, and has hardly built anything at all (Eversley 1975, 105). Other cities, that did show an almost Victorian boldness in the 1960s, have now descended into the same torpor under the combined influence of public expenditure cuts and the campaigns of the conservationists to save anything and everything. The illuminating force of civic leadership, it appears, is in danger of being snuffed out.

Future Scenarios

We now turn to the future. Will the trends, outlined in Chapter 2, persist from the 1960s and 1970s into the 1980s and 1990s? Or will the processes tend to weaken, and the inner cities reach some kind of equilibrium? Logically, out-movement of people and closure of industry cannot continue for ever; and it seems inherently implausible that they could continue until the whole city is emptied out. Might there not in any case be some major disjuncture that would upset all the smooth trend lines?

In order to explore such possibilities, clearly, simple extrapolation will not get us far. Rather, we need to speculate freely about the forces that might shape the inner city in relation to the wider metropolitan, regional, national and international forces of change. For such purposes, future forecasters have come to employ the method of scenario-writing: a mode that involves taking a systematic look at the possibilities under a number of subject headings, and then looking at their interrelationships, so as to obtain a range of synthesised possible futures.

Work to date

There has been a host of major exercises in scenario-writing in recent years. Fortunately, sixteen of the most significant have been ably summarised and systematically compared in a recent study by the Science Policy Research Unit at the University of Sussex (Freeman and Jahoda 1979). To their analysis we should append two other exercises in forecasting: the Europe 2000 study (Hall 1977a) and the Interfutures study commissioned by the Organisation for Economic Cooperation and Development (OECD 1979). What have all these studies to say about the likely future development of the inner city?

The answer, disconcertingly, is very little. This is because all these studies are deliberately focused at the macro or global scale. At most, they disaggregate down to the level of the nation state. They are concerned with questions like the future of industrial development in the Third World as compared with the First World; they do not address the industrial future of the inner city as compared with the suburbs or exurbs. Therefore, their use for us can be only indirect. They can be used to develop an understanding of broad forces, whose impact on the inner city we must explore for ourselves.

Even then it is not easy, because the scenarios differ so much among themselves. They take very different attitudes on such basic matters as resource constraints and likely levels of long-term economic growth, ranging from highly optimistic to highly pessimistic. They vary similarly on the very important dimension of income distribution: some assume a highly egalitarian world, others a highly inegalitarian one. They also differ fundamentally in their assumptions about how society will react to − or with − the forecast world, ranging from a conservative position (not too much intervention), through a reformist position (assuming that considerable intervention will prove acceptable and necessary), to a radical position (assuming that society will react through a major revolution in the structure of power). On this basis, the SPRU forecasters are able to classify each of their sixteen chosen forecasts along each of three dimensions, to create twelve possibilities in all (Freeman and Jahoda 1979, Chapter 8). The result of their discussion has been compressed and schematised in Table 7.1. Interestingly, it contains some examples in most of the cells − though in some cases the decision as to the most appropriate cell is a very fine one. Nevertheless it is clear that the dominant position, reflecting the major concerns of the 1970s, assumes low growth yet greater equality, involving a degree of social intervention.

The dominant view

What kind of world would result from this dominant group of scenarios? It would be a somewhat egalitarian world accepting an environmental ethos and a 'communal' style of society, with a general sense of satisfaction and equity. There would be an interest in self-achievement, craft and workmanship rather than status or recognition. There would be much concern with community medicine and distributive justice. There would be a stress on durability and quality in production, and in some industrialised countries there would, however, be unemployment. There would be a revival of traditional arts and leisure, and a development of local communications systems. Education might be oriented toward training in crafts and appreciation of ecology.

Table 7.1   Eighteen Forecasts Compared

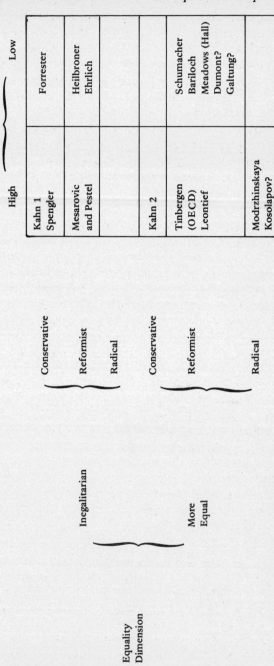

	Equality Dimension		Growth Dimensions	
			High	Low
Inegalitarian	Conservative		Kahn 1 Spengler	Forrester
	Reformist		Mesarovic and Pestel	Heilbroner Ehrlich
	Radical			
More Equal	Conservative		Kahn 2	
	Reformist		Tinbergen (OECD) Leontief	Schumacher Bariloch Meadows (Hall) Dumont? Galtung?
	Radical		Modrzhinskaya Kosolapov?	

Source: Freeman and Jahoda (1977); supplemented by Hall (1977a) and OECD (1979) which are shown in brackets.
(Note: Question marks means that there is a doubt as to the correct cell as this particular forecast).

In terms of built forms, the dominant scenario would involve a stress on conservation of energy and materials. Densities might be high to conserve transportation requirements, and there might be a good deal of renovation of older housing. However, it is not immediately clear whether the result would be a drift back to the cities, or an even more drastic deconcentration as people sought to live in smaller towns where distances were short and communication easier. It is possible that there would be a great deal of innovation in transportation systems, particularly involving the application of new technologies: for instance, information storage and processing to conserve energy or operate automated systems.

There is some uncertainty and disagreement, too, about the style of life and work within these built structures. Most assume that work patterns will be much improved, with job enrichment and job rotation, flexible working hours and technologies appropriate to work in small groups or alone – so that workers will be more free to choose their jobs (including a combination of different jobs) and their working hours more freely than today. Most agree, too, that there would be a better range of services – and some, though not all, assume that many of the jobs lost through industrial automation could be replaced by new service jobs. Certainly education should be much improved in both quantity and quality, particularly for the under-privileged, who will benefit from a vast increase in programmed learning and other distance-teaching technologies that make use of the new information systems. Similarly there would be a great extension of community organisations and services in fields like child care, health centres and social services. While some might be run by the state, there would probably be many innovations under private or charitable auspices (Freeman and Jahoda 1979, Chapter 9).

Effect on the inner city

To return to the critical point – it is far from clear what this dominant scenario, or indeed any scenario, would mean for the future of the inner city. Speculatively, it seems most likely that economic growth in the advanced industrial countries will be fairly heavily constrained down to the end of the century by energy and resource shortages, coupled with the challenge of newly industrialising countries. All this is likely to put a premium on the ability of any nation to compete through efficiency – which might be efficiency in the use of energy and materials, energy in the use of manpower, or a combination of the two. There may well be an acute clash here between the private balance of costs and benefits, that will suggest increased automation and labour shedding, and the social balance, that will suggest redeployment and work sharing.

Many of the scenarios — whether optimistic or pessimistic — also assume that certain stable industries (steel, ships, cars) are going to be threatened by a combination of weak secular growth of demand and competition from highly efficient newly industrialising countries (Korea, Singapore, Brazil, Mexico). This suggests that the right strategy for the advanced countries will be to get out of such ageing staples as fast as they can, developing instead such important new industries as electronics and micro-processors, the exploitation of energy and mining resources in the oceans, the development of new sources of energy, and — with less certainty — the bio-engineering industries (OECD 1979, 114-8; Sharp 1980, 378). However, it is clear that on their track record so far, the advanced countries have each very different prospects in these emerging areas. The United States and Japan, for instance, are very much better placed for growth in electronics than any other country, and Britain's prospects seem particularly dim (OECD 1979, 343).

For the inner cities of Britain, the message of such a scenario is far from comforting. As already suggested in Chapter 2, and reiterated here, it seems likely that the inner city has largely lost its innovative character, probably because its industrial milieu — dominated as it is by small and less-productive firms — is poor. This may be compounded by old plant and equipment and by negative characteristics among the labour force. Insofar as some inner city firms do produce technological innovation, that very fact may render them prone to take-over by other firms, especially multi-plant enterprises. Further, many inner city residents now work in relatively low-level service jobs, which are particularly open to capital substitution through technological innovation — especially through new information technologies depending on the microprocessor (Goddard and Thwaites 1980, 71-4). Firm evidence on these assumptions is so far lacking, and the pessimistic conclusions of Jenkins and Sherman (1979) have been challenged by Charles Cooper of the Science Policy Research Unit, who argues that micro-processors may spawn production innovations that may create more jobs than are lost by the process innovations they will undoubtedly bring. But, if the views of the pessimists have any point, then a low growth era — accompanied by tough international and inter-regional competition — would spell even worse trouble for the inner city: its poor competitive position would show up even more starkly, and it might survive only by maintaining a pool of poorly paid labour in competition with more innovative, more highly-capitalised units in other regions and in other countries.

Alternative Strategies
The foregoing, it must be stressed again, is all highly speculative. But speculation is all that is open to us. So to continue in this vein: what kinds of economic strategy, in these circumstances, might be open to British inner cities and to the people who manage and guide them?

Resurgence of industry
Traditionally in Britain manufacturing industry tended to prefer inner city locations: thus, precision instruments in London, jewellery and guns in Birmingham. But, as already suggested in Chapter 2, industry now seems to be deserting the inner cities for suburban and even rural centres. One reason could be that — just as in the United States — industry now prefers what Berry (1979, 1976) calls amenity-rich locations. Thus, it follows the preference of its skilled workforce for certain kinds of places in which to live, and at present the inner cities probably score just about bottom in their ranking. This suggests that it might just be possible to woo such industry back by a combination of policies: incentives to universities and polytechnics to set up spin-off industrial corporations (as has happened widely in the United States); incentives for innovative individuals, to encourage them to develop small industries in leading technological areas; skill training, to upgrade the local labour force and provide an appropriate labour pool; and specialised industrial parks together with appropriate housing and leisure facilities, to transform part at least of the inner city environment — such a policy appears to have worked extremely well, for instance, in the case of Birchwood industrial park in Warrington New Town. However, it should be stressed that in true inner city locations these solutions would involve the reversal of extremely powerful trends. They might be possible in one or two selected places, but overall the prospects are not very good.

The quarternary and quinary sectors
The second recipe would be to build up the inner city economy on the basis of the fast-growing quaternary sector (banking, insurance and finance business services) and what Bell (1973, Table 1.1, 117) calls the quinary sector (public services, including the mass media, consultancy and higher education). These are the true growth industries in all

industrialised countries, the typical activities of the post-industrial society. Many seem to show a continuing affinity to the central business districts of the largest cities, though admittedly, some have recently moved out to a variety of locations, including suburbs and small towns. These industries also tend to employ a remarkably wide spread of different kinds of workers — ranging from top managers and editors, professors and television producers, all the way to porters and cleaners. Further, the income and employment multipliers are once again high, so such industry can trigger off a broad-based growth in service industries.

The chief problem with this solution is that it may work for a very few cities (London, possibly Edinburgh) but perhaps not many others. There is some evidence that large-scale organisations in these sectors are tending to concentrate their activities in relatively few top-order cities on a European or even a world scale, thus deserting the second-order provincial capitals. And even in the biggest places, there tends to be a degree of decentralisation to satellite towns within the broad metro-politan sphere — as from New York to Stamford and New Haven, London to Reading or Basingstoke. Though formerly affecting the more routine kinds of office function, this is now taking top-level functions out of the big cities. If this movement spreads as a result of better communications — especially as a result of the microprocessor revolution — it could mean that once again the inner city will become almost the least favoured location. But this will depend in part on the locational preferences of key workers in this sector, to which we shall return.

Tourism

The third strategy is to develop an economy based on tourism together with associated services and manufacturing industries — including craft industry and associated shops and trade centres, and food processing. Tourism is one of the fastest-expanding industries in almost every country, though its prospects depend directly on the growth of dis-posable income, and so on the rate of economic development generally. Since the real cost of travel tends constantly to be reduced through a combination of technological development ('jumbos' and other wide-bodied jetliners) and organisational change (break-up of regulatory cartels), tourism in a country like Britain could benefit massively from economic growth in far distant countries (the newly-industrialising group) even if growth in nearer neighbours slowed down. Further, tourism has a natural affinity for some of the bigger capital cities, which are seen as repositories of history and cultural tradition as well as of entertainment.

This might suggest that again, such a solution could work for a London or an Edinburgh but not for a Liverpool or a Glasgow. However, tourism can also be generated through deliberate stimulation — as the very different examples of Birmingham's National Exhibition Centre and Florida's Walt Disney World will amply demonstrate. What is required above all is imagination — and some individuals in some inner cities doubtless have this. Once the triggering mechanism is created, then associated craft industry with showrooms can prove extremely effective in re-invigorating old, run-down warehouse areas in or near the city centres, like London's Covent Garden. Tourist cities by their nature are likely to attract entrepreneurial individuals and thus to spin off further industries. Finally, tourism does create an extremely wide spectrum of employment, including many unskilled service jobs that are not so likely to be displaced by technological advance — even if they tend to be low-paying jobs in less pleasant conditions.

Foreign investment

There is yet a further strategy. It is to recognise that in the period when inner city innovation did flourish, it did so to a remarkable degree with the aid of newly-arrived groups of people who brought with them a strong entrepreneurial tradition. The Huguenots in London in the seventeenth century, the Jews at the end of the nineteenth, the Indians in our day, all provide examples. The same might happen again, if we attracted small businessmen, with capital and expertise, to settle and establish small workshops and trading centres. Thus we might begin to emulate the drive and enthusiasm of emerging centres like Singapore or Hongkong. Witness, in the second half of the 1970s, the development of London's Tottenham Court Road as a rival electronics trading centre to Hongkong's Nathan Road. True, the immediate result might be some decline in the standards of hygiene and safety in industrial premises. Perhaps, it may be argued, this is a classic case where the best, in the form of central government and local authority regulation, may be the enemy of the good in terms of job creation. Such notions provided the original basis for the concept of the Enterprise Zone (Hall 1977b) which, in much transmuted form, has now been embodied in British governmental policy.

This is of course a drastic policy that could not be adopted very widely. It might be seen as a last-ditch solution for the worst-afflicted areas like parts of London's dockland or inner Liverpool, where much of the land is derelict and most of the jobs have gone. The modified version of the strategy is simply to encourage small firms to develop in the inner city, by trying to remove some of the obstacles they now find in starting and growing. Policies to this end might include provision of small ready-to-let industrial workshops, generally through conversion of older industrial and warehouse buildings, but also through small purpose-built factories on industrial estates; provision of common services, such as marketing or accountancy, for small firms that could not afford these on an individual basis; and loans or grants to small businesses that lack the established reputation to get conventional finance.

Government policy, through the urban programmes and the partnerships, has aided local authority provision of small workshops, while the voluntary sector has also made some interesting experiments that could be repeated far more widely. And the modified version of the Enterprise Zones, introduced by the Conservative Government in 1980, offers further inducements in certain areas that could be particularly attractive to small firms: tax concessions, freedom from detailed planning requirements, simplified statistical reporting procedures and exemption from training levies. All these might help. The Enterprise Zones in particular must be viewed as laboratory experiments in social science, that may succeed or may not. The evidence is contradictory as to whether such factors as planning and other controls are really inhibiting industrial growth in the inner city; we can but try to find out.

Still, we should not be too optimistic. Despite efforts by successive governments, ever since the Bolton report (Committee on Small Firms 1971) the evidence has been compelling that the small industry sector in Britain has been poorly developed in comparison with other countries, and is declining. The causes may lie very deep, at a level not easily open to government policy levers. For instance, entrepreneurship appears to be weak generally in Britain, and this weakness may be particularly concentrated in inner city locations from which the more entrepreneurial individuals have fled. Thus government policy shifts may achieve some effect at the margin, by tempting some individuals or firms to locate in inner city locations rather than elsewhere, but they are less likely to engender completely new economic activity where none existed before. Unless this vicious circle can somehow be broken, more and more of the generation of new activity is likely to pass into the hands of the bigger industrial corporations, and — as already seen in Chapter 2 — they are not prone to make a major locational shift back into the inner cities — rather the reverse.

Society, Culture and Lifestyle

Closely associated with these locational decisions — whether by small entrepreneurs or the executives of big companies — is the critical question of physical and social milieu. If the Berry hypothesis is correct for Britain as well as for the United States, then economic activity will increasingly be drawn to amenity-rich locations that reflect the locational preferences of key sections of the workforce. (This, it is important to note, does not reflect a triumph of purely social over economic factors; it can be economically rational, if the right kinds of labour are easier to attract in these locations.) In the United States, the typical run-down inner city has come to represent almost the very worst kind of environment in the eyes of most people; hence the efforts of cities like Detroit and St. Louis to create a totally new physical ambience in their central areas. But the problem goes deeper than physical reconstruction: it is a matter also of social preferences for kinds of housing, kinds of neighbours, kinds of schools, kind of social activity — in other words, the total lifestyle.

A history of decline

Rapidly in the United States after World War Two, perhaps more belatedly and more slowly in Great Britain, the inner city started to fail to meet the demands of many aspirant people for a style of life that they felt they wanted for themselves and their children. These people perceived its housing stock as too old and too run down, its general physical environment as too shoddy, careworn and depressing, its street system too old and congested to meet the needs of car owners, its public transport system expensive and deteriorating. More than this, immigration of new groups into inner city areas often brought social stresses, as cultural traditions and lifestyles failed to mesh, while educational standards in inner city schools were perceived as poor and even declining. Given the general middle class norms of the 1950s and 1960s — in favour of a standard familistic lifestyle based on child rearing and the family — it was small wonder that in both countries, millions left the cities in search of homes in suburbia (Overton, 1980).

In the 1970s and 1980s, the position in both countries is more complex. On the one hand, in many ways the plight of the cities is worse even than before. The remaining stock of older housing is very likely to deteriorate progressively with age, as its owners, often old and with low incomes, fail to maintain it. The mass urban renewal of the 1960s paradoxically brings further problems since the new stock, hastily built to unsuitable designs, begins to show rapid obsolescence and decay. The general physical milieu remains very poor and is compounded by cuts in public expenditure which reduce the level of maintenance of buildings and streets. New problems are beginning to appear such as the almost simultaneous decay of the vast Victorian network of infrastructure under the streets. Social dislocation, arising from the problems of socialisation of the first generation of children of the immigrants of the 1960s, brings further problems. Rising car ownership — albeit less rapid than before the oil crisis of 1973—4, and from a lower level here than elsewhere in the country — causes further problems of congestion and frustration on the streets, while the public transport system — hit by cuts in subsidies — plunges towards financial crisis.

A possible revival?

On the other hand, there is now the possibility of a new counter-force. American experience, if it is a guide — and often in the past, it has proved to be — suggests that certain social and demographic changes are working strongly in favour of the inner city again. They are closely associated: they include the strength of the women's liberation movement, a rejection of the idea of marriage among many young people, the greater stress on professional careers for women as well as men, a strong rejection of child bearing and child rearing expressed in a drastic reduction of the birth rate, and a dramatic increase in divorce rates leading to the formation of new households in middle age. Associated with this is the entry into adulthood of the 'suburban generation' of children of the 1950s and 1960s, with an apparent revulsion on the part of many against the lifestyle of their parents — and even a rejection of suburbia by these same parents, especially if divorce brings a radical disjuncture in life patterns. All this is leading to a rediscovery of the American city by a new generation of young, professional, high-income households which have no (or few) children, and generally consist of one or two people. The movement — labelled officially 'neighborhood revitalization', but widely recognised by the British word 'gentrification' — has now spread from its original strongholds in the bigger, more attractive service industry centres, to embrace some parts of almost every major city: thus Baltimore as well as Washington, Pittsburgh as well as Philadelphia. The process is admittedly very patchy: islands of gentrification exist in the midst of poverty and decay.

In Britain so far, it appears that the process is more muted. It is very marked in London, less so in many other cities, hardly noticeable at all in some. The social groups that are spearheading the American process are not so well represented in Britain. Higher education, and the patterns of social interaction associated with it, are much less well developed in Britain and the prospects for further growth do not seem bright. With less highly developed upper-middle class seeking a highly interactive, cosmopolitan lifestyle, the suburban and small town trend in Britain may prove to continue to be the dominant one. For middle range managers, for clerical workers and for skilled manual workers such places do provide the 'good city' for their families and especially for the education of their children (Donnison and Soto, 1980, Chs. 8 and 10 *passim*). In any event, it is important to notice that in the United States, the process has in no way stemmed the outward flow of people from the cities. Paradoxically, as with gentrification in London, it has exacerbated the problem, as the new middle-class urbanites occupy more space than the poorer people they displaced.

So, on fairly conservative scenarios, the future for the inner cities looks much like the recent past. Failing a radical disjuncture of some kind, their economy is likely to continue to decay as large firms nationalise and shut down older plants, and as new small entrepreneurs fail to arise to fill the gap. The most promising types of future for inner city economies — such as tourism or immigrant small industry — are also likely to involve quite low wages, long or irregular hours, and perhaps poor working conditions. Nor will the physical and social ambience of the inner city prove very attractive to the great majority of ordinary people who have any kind of freedom to decide where to live and work. The people who remain in the inner city are increasingly likely to be those who are trapped there by reason of the kind of job they do, the kind of housing they occupy, or their lack of proper information about alternatives. A minority of colonising intellectuals and professionals, in London and perhaps one or two other places, is unlikely to prove much of an exception to this rule.

Technological Factors
Energy conservation
If there are any forces that might upset the trend scenarios it is most likely that they are technological in character. One is that real energy costs would rise rapidly, forcing a substantial reduction in personal mobility. Long-distance commuting in particular would be greatly cut back. There would be a premium on compact patterns of living and working. Here — as usual — there is much disagreement among the experts. A careful recent review of all the evidence concludes that there

will be no problem of physical availability of energy on Earth at least for the next hundred years, though there are major uncertainties about the ultimately recoverable resources of oil and natural gas — so that there is a strong case for conserving them for premium uses. However, the scope for conservation measures is very considerable, so that — along with greater use of coal as compared with oil and gas, plus a cautious development of nuclear reactors and hydro, wind, solar and geothermal sources — there should be no real restraint on world growth (Freeman and Jahoda, 1978, Chapter 5).

This is comforting, but one of the more important modes of conservation considered in this review is 'the possibilities for redesigning cities, towns, and transport systems so as to reduce drastically the demand for road transport' especially through a reduction in private car travel (Freeman and Jahoda, 1978, 140). The problem is that this solution would run right up against the established preferences of consumers, and so could be enforced only through a drastic impact first on optional (leisure, social, and holiday) trips rather than on the journey to work, which for the great majority is not very long anyway. All in all, the most likely outcome would seem to be that a major increase in energy costs would be followed (or even preceded) by development of new forms of fuel-efficient cars, or by a downward trading of big cars for smaller ones, or both. In the United States it has been estimated that design improvements to cars could yield total savings of 20–40 percent (Freeman and Jahoda, 1978, 140), though in Europe the potential savings may be less. There might be some reduction in optional trips and a reduction in longer commuter trips, which would however not be very significant in the overall picture. Insofar as there were any effect on the patterns of cities and towns, it might consist of an even greater movement out of larger cities into smaller or medium-sized ones where average distances for all journey purposes were shorter. The notion that energy shortages will save the inner city, therefore, is probably a dangerous myth.

The information revolution

The other important technological possibility — and a far more likely, even certain one — is the rapid development of a new generation of information processing machines in the 1980s and 1990s, which many forecasters believe will constitute an 'information revolution' equal in its impact to the first industrial revolution based on electricity and the internal combustion engine. These previous revolutions saw an early growth phase, as new industries took advantage of the new technology,

followed by a depression as consumer demand failed to keep pace with
technological growth. Perhaps even more relevant to this discussion,
new technologies tend to diffuse unevenly: some industries and groups
and individuals gain tremendous advantages from early entry, and these
may be located in particular places which will also gain thereby
(Goddard and Thwaites, 1980, 63-4).

The new technology, Goddard and Thwaites suggest, is likely to have
three main impacts. First there will be a whole range of new industrial
products in which microelectronics form a major component. These
will probably displace older technologies (mechanical telephone
exchanges, speedometers, and other gauges, and many others) with
quite drastic effects on some localities. Further, the new electronic
industries are likely to appear in different places from the old because
they will tend to seek 'amenity-rich' locations for their top staff. The
inner cities, as stressed earlier, are unlikely to prove very competitive on
that count.

Second, there are process innovations concerning the way in which
goods are made or services are provided. In manufacturing, robots and
large-scale automation are likely to eliminate many skilled jobs but to
create other skilled jobs. The spatial impacts are difficult to assess, but
Goddard and Thwaites suggest that the main effect will be felt in areas
with a large skill input into production, like Sheffield steel and the metal
working industries of the East and West Midlands. More important could
be the process innovations in the service industries, through computeris-
ation and, above all, office automation. The biggest impacts here will
probably be on routine clerical jobs, which are highly concentrated in
the biggest metropolitan areas, especially Liverpool and Newcastle. There
could however be some dampening of this effect if — as seems to have
been the case so far — the peripheral regions are relatively slow in taking
up the innovations. Lastly, there could be displacement of skilled
workers, too — as in the obvious example of the publishing and printing
of newspapers (Goddard and Thwaites 1980, 67—9).

Thirdly, Goddard and Thwaites suggest, there will be effects upon
managerial innovation: the new technologies will open up new possibilities for the management of organisations. In particular, increasingly
sophisticated telecommunications could substitute for face-to-face
contact and personal movement. Currently, in many organisations the
top-level managerial functions seem to be increasingly concentrated in
the larger cities — not merely on a national, but also on an international
scale. Only the lower-level functions are left in the regions, and their
more routine contacts can be substituted by telecommunications,

leading to the opportunity for even more remote control. On the other hand, top management meetings are more substitutable by telecommunications, suggesting that these functions could be decentralised. However, as lower-level management is often concerned with the actual production process, the most logical system would seem to involve top management using telecommunications to control manufacturing from a remote headquarters (Goddard and Thwaites 1980, 54). But the use of telecommunications is more difficult in the service sector and it is this sector that is most highly concentrated in the South East (Goddard and Thwaites 1980, 54).

The studies that have taken place so far are however of limited value in studying the inner city, because they deal with inter-regional issues. Goddard and Thwaites suggest that office functions in manufacturing industry are likely to follow the production plants out of the inner cities and into suburban or exurban locations, while service office functions that have traditionally occupied central locations because of the need to draw on a large labour pool (insurance, banking and finance, and public administration) may experience big substitution of capital for labour. So the implications of the electronic management revolution for the inner city economy do not look good.

All in all, then, major technological changes in the coming decades seem most unlikely to work in favour of the inner city – if anything, the reverse. The most likely scenario by far is one of continued, even accelerated decline and of a greater concentration of deprived people – particularly since the skills demanded to operate the new technologies are likely to be least present among inner city residents. Indeed the fear must be that large parts of the higher-level tertiary and quaternary sectors will join the manufacturing and routine clerical functions in the flight from the city. The chief remaining functions of the inner city would then seem to lie in relatively unskilled and low-paid jobs in tourism and in immigrant industry, with perhaps remaining concentrations of higher-order functions in a small handful of major cities.

However, the process would not end there. In such circumstances, it would be very plausible to postulate what Marxists call the marginalisation of the inner city population. The unskilled and the undereducated, increasingly unable to compete, would be thrown out of regular work almost permanently or would never even enter it. Trades unions would actually encourage this development in their desire to protect the jobs of their existing members. The plight of such people would of course be mitigated, in a country like Britain, by the strong ideological links between trades unions and leftist parties that would put curbs on union power, together with the obligations of governments to maintain at least a minimal basis of social services. Nevertheless, there is a very real prospect of the development, within a predominantly affluent and also enlightened society, of a substantial minority of poor, frustrated, alienated and dysfunctional groups who could present a source of grave social malaise. The experience of the United States indicates that such phenomena — expressed in indices such as crime, drug abuse, family breakdown and educational drop-out — have been to a large degree concentrated in the inner cities. If British cities followed the same path, and there are indications of this, then the prospects for any economic regeneration would be even slimmer (Hall 1977a, 71—2, 223).

These are powerful trends. They could be reversed only if there were some quite fundamental transformation of the basis of the inner city economy — a transformation that is not merely economic or technological, but social and cultural in character. Though this is inherently unlikely in the short run, it should cause us to pose the question: what are the deep underlying forces that help shape the fortunes of cities and regions at different periods of time? That question is addressed in the final chapter.

Some Unanswered Questions

From this review of the past and future, two main research priorities emerge. The first is to try to make some bridge between the excessively global and general long-term future forecasting exercises that have been briefly compared in this chapter, and the excessively narrow and short-term economic forecasting exercises relating to Britain in particular. To understand the inner city in its total context, we need a set of alternative scenarios that develop a model of the world economy into which the British inner city will fit. For, as has repeatedly been stressed in this book, the fate of our cities will be determined not so much in town halls or in the Department of the Environment headquarters, as by decisions taken in other parts of Britain and other parts of the world. Until we understand the constraints which these decisions will post to our freedom of action, we cannot begin to gauge which policies are feasible and which are likely to be helpful.

Secondly, within that framework we want to begin to appreciate the forces that control the economic resilience of a city or a region. Though external forces are strong, they do not impose some predetermined economic fate. Cities may rise or fall by the efforts, or lack of effort, of their own entrepreneurs and their own city fathers. We want to understand the forces of innovative growth, and for that reason we should be studying the successful cases rather than those that now seem to be failures. To these themes we return in Chapter 8.

8   A Research Agenda
Peter Hall and Derek Diamond

This final chapter tries to set out the essential conclusions from our study of what is now known about the inner city and its problems, and on that basis to suggest an agenda for further research. But we must start by stressing that this is not a digest of the findings of the entire study. They are too rich and too diverse for ready summary. Rather, we present here a highly selective account of those findings which appear to us to be the most important for further research. We try to outline those questions that seem crucial, yet are still not illuminated by research in depth. As will soon be seen, these questions go far beyond the limits of the inner city in any conventional sense. Indeed, our most important conclusion — and our basic stance — can be stated straight-away: *We do not believe that the inner city, as such, is the most helpful research focus.* It will prove a useful starting point, but over-concentration on it will run the risk of missing the main point, which is this: *Inner city areas can best be understood as phenomena resulting from underlying forces in the British economy and society*, including the international context, interacting with specific conditions prevailing in large urban areas to produce diverse outcomes, conventionally labelled the inner city problem. The inner city problem is thus a caricature of the forces affecting urban areas: Our concern throughout is to identify those forces.

An exclusive inner city focus is misconceived and misleading in another way: it does not sufficiently recognise the fact that these older urban areas are highly diverse. That in turn is because they are integrated in space and in time with the rest of the economy. What are conventionally regarded as inner city problems — unemployment, bad housing, population decline, poverty — are not found in all inner city areas; neither are they exclusive to inner cities. They are due in large part to forces of change external to any one area, which then interact with forces specific to each inner city, to produce distinctively different results in each one. For this reason, what conventional accounts call inner city problems, we prefer to call symptoms; and we are concerned at the continued use of the conventional label. The danger is that it gives unjustified credence to purely locational explanations, and places unjustified hope on policy instruments that are narrowly defined in terms of particular areas. In turn it may divert social research from the important task of examining the macro changes and their structural causes, and thus put policy-makers in an even weaker position to understand and cope with the changes of the future.

Put another way, our work suggests that research should be concerned to understand the forces of change that are altering the fortunes of people and their workplaces in cities and towns in contemporary Britain and may alter them even more drastically and suddenly in the years ahead. Many of the processes of change studied by social scientists — for example in the labour or housing markets — operate within spatial settings with distinctive characteristics, which are crucial to the way in which the processes themselves operate. Many of the so-called rigidities in British society have a specific local and spatial dimension. We are concerned with both the direction of change and the rate of change. Behind that, we are concerned with the causes of change, and the way they interact, and the ways in which areas respond to these challenges. These causes, as analysed in our reading of the literature, are very varied. They range from structural and technological change in the economy to ageing infrastructure in and under the streets, from an altering age structure of the population to a wide range of changing preferences — including for example the location of homes and workplaces, the nature of work and of marriage, and of style of government.

In essence, our method of working has been to ask, for each of the main subject areas selected for review: first, what is happening; secondly, why it is happening; thirdly, how significant it is; fourthly, how apt are the policy responses; and fifthly, how likely will future change be. We recognise that change comes from extremely varied causes, and that the relative importance of these causes tends to vary a great deal from case to case. This is bound to create real difficulties in choosing research priorities and in completing the research itself. Some of the analyses we have examined tend to limit the search for causes to an artificially narrow area, and so to stress specifically 'urban explanations'. Thus resident characteristics are examined to explain unemployment, and the characteristics of inner city firms are examined to account for industrial decline. Also, with a few honourable exceptions, research has tended to ignore the nature of the interrelationships between the diverse processes, especially where these are difficult to identify empirically. So, in order to overcome the piecemeal bias of previous work, within our research priorities we give top place to the large-scale and the multi-faceted.

This approach leads us to believe that priority should be given to two kinds of study. First, those conducted within broad spatial frameworks; these would make systematic comparisons between carefully-chosen diverse locations, each with specific bundles of characteristics, with the aim of developing a general understanding of how areas of different types behave. We should ask how far the contemporary careers of cities, towns and countrysides reflect exogenous influences and how far endogenous ones. Such knowledge would then be compared with future scenarios having different rates and components of social and economic change. These global or structural trends would also embody different national and local policy responses, thus allowing some judgement about their longer-term consequences for different kinds of area.

Secondly, and relatedly, other studies would link the perspectives and methodologies of different disciplines with the specific aim of understanding better how causes interact. For example, what is the nature of the relationship between industrial restructuring through mergers, technological innovations and their diffusion, and changing perceptions of what constitutes an adequate working environment? And what might be the combined impact of all these on particular kinds of areas? Questions of this kind need insights from economics, organisational behaviour, location and perception studies, to quote only a few.

It follows from this that the research effort should concentrate on key processes, in particular the interdependence of economic, social, physical and political factors on the spirals of investment/disinvestment and the exploration of this interdependence in the differing milieux of different cities and countrysides.

Structural Change and the Local Economy

One of the most critical causes of change in the British space economy is the effect of *structural change*. For a long time this economy has been growing sluggishly, compared with its neighbours and competitors. There is strong evidence that it is not proving competitive within a world economy and even that this failure is worsening. Overseas industrial nations, including both our older-established European neighbours and the newer industrialising nations of East and South East Asia and elsewhere, are achieving increased import penetration; and our export performance does not improve to compensate. Productivity is low and the rate of innovation — above all in leading sectors — appears poor.

The international dimension is exacerbated by a second factor: the *technological* one. There is clear evidence that British industry is less highly capitalised, that its plants and machinery are older and in poorer condition, than many of our competitors, above all the newly-industrialising nations. The same may be true of the tertiary sector: in the age of the word processor, many British offices are not even equipped with electric typewriters. Ironically, this failure to invest in technology may protect workers from displacement and unemployment for some time — but at the cost of lower productivity and lower wages than would otherwise be the case. The challenge of the microprocessor may be seized by other economies, leaving us behind once again.

This poor competitive performance also has a third, *sectoral* dimension. Britain's performance in some manufacturing sectors, such as motor vehicles and electronics, has been extremely disappointing. In others, such as certain kinds of specialised scientific equipment, it has been more encouraging. In some tertiary industries, such as finance, the media, consulting, professional services and specialised services such as software, it has been highly competitive in world terms — and these are predominant among the few industries providing employment growth in the British economy in the last decade. But these growing and declining sectors tend to be concentrated in different regions and different cities, even different parts of cities, so the process has a spatial dimension.

There is a serious risk that in the 1980s this failure will come to affect a widening part of total British output, threatening previous regional comparative advantage and removing the jobs of whole groups and whole areas — skilled craftsmen, managers, the West Midlands and parts of the South East — formerly thought to be immune. Similarly, the sudden impact of the new technologies may destroy large numbers of jobs in just those sectors and just those areas where expansion has been greatest over the last thirty years — in female clerical labour and in the prosperous towns of the South East, for instance. All this could have sudden and drastic results on the fortunes of individuals and families. Already only one British region — the South East — enjoys above-average incomes in EEC terms. The threatened further changes could turn Britain into a vast underdeveloped area in Europe.

A fourth dimension of structural change concerns *ownership and control*. The weak competitive position of many industries has encouraged the process of take-over by stronger and better-organised competitors, often multi-plant and even multi-national companies. This process of rationalisation and concentration has led to the closure of the less competitive, often older and less well-equipped, plants – some of which have been in the older, inner parts of the conurbations. Ironically, regional policy may have encouraged this process through its emphasis on capital grants and allowances. Low-skill, low-pay jobs – especially in manufacturing – tend to be concentrated in peripheral regions where they are very vulnerable to change, while the limited pool of high-skill jobs – in managerial and professional occupations and generally in the tertiary sector – becomes increasingly concentrated in the South East, especially that part of it outside Greater London. Though this picture of 'regional polarisation' of the British economy should not be accepted without question, it definitely demands further research. In particular, work is needed on the internal dynamics of those declining peripheral regions, such as Central Scotland, that are dependent on a central urban core, itself in decline.

Against this background, it is now possible to spell out some research priorities. There is probably no need for substantial expansion of research into the macro-future of the British economy. Existing work in short-to-medium-range forecasting at NIESR, at the London Business School, and at the Department of Applied Economics at Cambridge, all now supported by SSRC, will continue. But there is a strong case for extending it into the medium-to-long-range period. This will involve alternative scenarios based on various assumptions. Following on that, we should seek to develop some exercises in forecasting at a more micro-scale. We could ask, for instance, what would be the impact of a postulated collapse of BL on the economy of Birmingham and Coventry. This would mean looking rather specifically at the *processes* operating in the economy at different spatial scales – a focus that is missing in the macro-economic modelling approach. It is also necessarily missing from the Department of the Environment's more narrowly-focused programme of applied research, which our own programme would complement.

Aspects of Change:
The large firm and city decline
There is an important need to focus on certain processes of structural change and their interrelationships. Very significant in this respect is the behaviour of the individual entrepreneur – especially the larger corporate entrepreneur, whose tendency to desert inner city locations

is particularly important. We do not yet know for instance whether this shift is due to a fall in the private rate of return earned by capital there; whether it is a temporary adjustment phenomenon, associated with the age of capital stock; whether the level of incentives is of any significance, given that most of the seriously declining urban economies have been (and are still) in the Special Development Area category; or whether other factors — such as congestion, high land costs, poor industrial relations or a generally depressing environment — are of greater importance. Lastly, we need specifically to consider whether — especially for these larger corporations — the inner city still represents an attractive location for certain kinds of new industries and services. This may involve a study not merely of productive corporations, but also of speculative developers of offices and other commercial buildings. We know little, in particular, about the operation of the city land market, about the identity of the key investors, or the forces that shape their investment decisions, or about their possible response to incentives.

The small firm in the inner city — and elsewhere

In parallel, we need to look also at the small firm — not every small firm, but those that are fairly young and dynamic. A wealth of recent literature suggests that the inner areas of large industrial cities represent a kind of soft under-belly of the British economy, feeling most intensely the shocks that affect the economy as a whole. One principal reason for this is that many firms, especially smaller ones, are ageing — though the death rate may not indeed by higher than elsewhere. The problem is that the inner cities seem to have a lower than average birth rate for new manufacturing firms and also for new firms in tertiary industry. This is a strange fact when it is recalled that historically the inner cities were regarded as the seedbeds of innovation and entrepreneurship. Some evidence indeed suggests that parts of the inner city no longer present an appropriate milieu for the development of new firms, and innovation flourishes most in smaller or medium-sized towns in rural regions. (It is even suggested that the prevalence of such towns in France and Germany may provide a clue to the higher rate of innovation there.) At any rate, it is known from much research — most notably that for the Bolton Committee in 1971 (Committee on Small Firms 1971) — that our small firms provide a smaller proportion of employment and output than in other major industrial countries such as Germany and the United States — and that this disproportion may be worsening.

Recent evidence — from the important MIT study by Birch — strongly suggests that in the United States smaller firms are disproportionately responsible for the creation of new jobs, and this alone may provide a clue for the poor performance of British industry in general and selected inner city areas in particular (Birch 1979, *passim*). However, the American work entirely fails to disaggregate manufacturing from service firms, and its results may reflect an institutional environment — in terms of financial and managerial barriers to entry, or the lack of them — that is not replicated in Britain. We therefore need to build on the limited amount of work at present underway in this country, with particular stress on policy variations that could affect the success rate of the young small firm. Here, as elsewhere, our position is not deterministic: structural change does provide a set of serious challenges, and may limit freedom of choice in response, but does nevertheless leave a field of action for imaginative policies.

The process of birth and growth of small-scale industry must clearly provide one of our major research foci. But it will be important here to study the relationships between small-scale and large-scale industry. Evidence from some urban economies suggests that small firms act mainly as suppliers of goods and specialised services to larger ones, and are highly dependent on the existence of a few large plants. However, there is also evidence that this type of relationship is more weakly developed in Britain, since here larger firms have attained a greater degree of vertical integration. But this may vary from industry to industry and from city to city; it certainly demands more sustained attention.

The Urban Milieu

Whether we are concerned with the disappearance of large firms or the failure of small ones to appear to take their place, the critical explanation may well be that certain kinds of area no longer represent an appropriate milieu for the expanding kinds of economic activity — whether in manufacturing or, still more, the expanding tertiary industries. But the poor milieu of some localities may mean more than simply a lack of entrepreneurs. For in addition the social milieu may be hostile, in terms of attitudes to risk and innovation. Moreover, coupled with this, the local political milieu may be heavily biased towards traditional economic remedies that are no longer viable. Cities may in other words have 'careers', in some phases of which they are young and adaptive, in others old and inflexible. But it appears *prima facie* that some cities, even very old ones, may retain youth and flexibility over centuries — or even regain these qualities after losing them. Bristol in the nineteenth century lost the Atlantic trade to Liverpool because of its conservatism and short-sightedness, but now Bristol booms while Liverpool stagnates.

All this suggests that a central research priority should be to focus on the conditions for economic success through innovation, adaptation, and new-firm growth. *Instead of concentrating solely on the woes of Britain's problem cities, we should focus attention on the economic successes, both here and abroad.* For in that way we may hope to define more precisely what it is that the failures have lacked — and so define the preconditions for making them successful again.

There are a number of research priorities under this heading. First, we should look closely at the conditions of formation and growth of new firms, especially in the technologically-advanced sectors. We should look at individual firm histories and at the obstacles to their growth and how these were overcome. Second and parallel to this, we should study at a slightly more macro level the individual fortunes of towns and regions, paying special attention to those cities that seem to have been continuously successful (York, Edinburgh, Leicester, Reading). We should ask what it is, whether in the entrepreneurial atmosphere, the socioeconomic composition or the political attitudes of the local council, that helped produce this success. These studies should not be narrowly economic but also sociological and political, and they might well draw on insights from social anthropology. For it may be that we are dealing with questions of cultural milieu that will be difficult to tease out in any other terms. Thirdly, we should extend these comparisons to our major industrial competitors, studying the innovative experiences of France and Germany. Our aim would be to study a wide range of comparative bases, both the successful ones and — to provide a control — the unsuccessful ones. Thus we might compare the experiences of Bristol and Liverpool, Hamburg and Glasgow. The object would be to find what it is in the cultural milieu that generates adaptability in one city, but fails to do so in another.

Adjustment in the Labour Market

Changes in the nature of the space economy, in response to the structural processes described in the preceding section, can also be examined at a more micro level. Developments in the spatial structure of urban areas interact with the exogenous forces of change to produce an altering 'structure of opportunity' within each town. Our review of the literature powerfully suggests that there is a complex — and so far poorly understood — set of relationships between migration, job opportunities, housing availability, skill acquisition, and household structure. Some age and skill groups are still relatively highly mobile, others much less so. This may reflect partly the availability of certain types of work, partly the effect of age and family structure on migration potential, and partly the effect of housing tenure (even if the skilled manual worker in a council flat were minded to move for a better job — or for any job at all — he would find it difficult to do so for housing reasons). It is clear that the lower-paid and lower-skilled workers are the least mobile, despite questionnaire evidence that many would like to move. Equally, it is clear that this group does not — or cannot — react to unemployment, or restricted job opportunities, by travelling long distances to work. The volume of reverse commuting from the conurbations is still negligible. Examination of the interaction between travel to work and skill or training involves both motivational studies and spatial analysis, as recent work on labour mobility demonstrates.

All this suggests a concentrated look at the recent patterns and characteristics of the movers and the stayers — both in terms of migration and in terms of commuting. We need to focus just as much on the implications for employment income and job satisfaction for those who do move as for those who stay put. But in this we also need to consider the final element in the jigsaw: the possibility of upgrading skills *in situ*, by formal or other means. Here there is a powerful suggestion that the government's Skillcentres may be poorly located in relation to the distribution of the least skilled and the most vulnerable.

Especially within the conurbations, there is a need to study the phenomenon of local labour markets — the areas within which workers will normally look for work. At any one moment these are fixed absolutely by the time and money that members of the labour force are willing and able to expend on the journey to work, but may also be constrained by their perceptions of employment opportunities. A very large conurbation like London may not be by any means a single local labour market in this sense, particularly for the less-skilled and lower-paid occupational groups: in the economic jargon, they may have tight spatial indifference curves. Thus in such a conurbation, it might be that some areas form favourable milieux for innovation and creation of new firms in the formal sector, while other areas do not (Central and West London versus East and South London); but that workers in the declining areas do not seek work in the developing ones, either because they do not perceive that it is available or because they do not think it is worth the time and trouble of the journey. If they do not travel, the question arises as to their responses: do they depend on welfare benefit, or do they (alternatively or additionally) join one facet or another of the informal economy? This question is likely to become rapidly more topical if, as we suppose, large additional groups of workers — especially in the under-21 and the over-50 group — become unemployed.

Another major focus for research, therefore, would be on the process of adaptation of the labour force. We need to ask:

(1) whether the educational and training potential of inner city school-leavers is any nearer being realised now than when the Educational Priority Areas were created, and if not, what are the obstacles in terms of institutions, personal discrimination, inadequacies of teachers of their training;

(2) how far and by what means can the mismatch between local labour supply and demand be reduced through altering the character of the supply, i.e. through education and training;

(3) whether the programmes of the Department of Employment and the Manpower Services Commission have improved the operation of local labour markets, either by better identification of local job opportunities, retraining, or assistance in moving to job opportunities;

(4) how far travel-to-work costs represent a barrier, or alternatively how far the problem is one of perception of job opportunities in geographical space;

(5) whether there are institutional barriers to the achievement of these policies.

The labour market in the formal economy is only one (albeit the major) part of the way in which households and individuals get and retain income. If a person becomes unemployed his income may be derived from welfare, or from work outside the conventional employment category which may be in cash or in kind, or from both. The relationship between employment, which by definition is paid, work, which may be paid or unpaid, and income, which may come either from employment or from other sources such as social welfare, is already highly complex. With shifting boundary lines, it is likely to become even more so in the next few years, especially in structural unemployment shows a rapid increase. We would therefore regard research in this field as of considerable importance.

The Informal Economy

Sociological and anthropological researchers have recently devoted much attention to the informal economy (Pahl and Geshuny 1980, 7–9). This showed that the informal economy in fact covers a variety of aspects ranging from the household economy (work done without reward), 'communal production' (outside households but also not for money) and 'hidden production' (for a money income, but not declared as such). The key is to understand the relationship between formal economic activity and all these kinds of informal activity. We need to understand how work gets transferred between the two; how work in the informal economy is distributed by sex, age, and class; and what may be the impact of public policies on the size and character of the informal economy. There is a suggestion here that the boundary between the two economies is a very flexible and constantly shifting one. In periods of rising unemployment and diminishing opportunities in the formal sector, the informal sector – bolstered, to be sure, by social security and other welfare payments from the formal sector – may expand to fill the gap. And it may be that this is why, so far, high rates of unemployment have failed to generate the evident distress and sense of outrage that characterised the early 1930s. But equally, the capacity to shift into the informal economy may vary as between one kind of urban milieu and another. We simply do not know how far the informal economy provides a kind of cushion against the failing of the formal economy in different sizes and kinds of cities.

This suggests at least two major research avenues. First, more work is needed to estimate the scale and distribution of informal economic activities – through the use of time budgets, and through sample surveys of people's provenance of goods and services; and second, we need investigations into the impact of unemployment on individuals, households, and local communities. The focus needs to be on the subtle and shifting relationship between the formal and the informal economy for different groups of people. Many individuals may well belong in both, for most or all of the time: the self-employed and artisans certainly do. This is particularly important, because it may contribute to our understanding of how we can encourage the revitalisation of localities through more entrepreneurial activity. Such activity is most likely to come from precisely those groups that find themselves in the area of overlap between the two economies.

Small-scale entrepreneurs may also be discouraged by planning and other regulations – for instance, health and safety or employment protection regulation. Certainly, there is evidence from other parts of the world that they tend to flourish where legislation is rudimentary and its regulation is lax. All this suggests that the right way to approach the problem may be through a very intensive field study of small — especially 'informal' — enterprises and their linkages, using methods of social anthropology whereby the researcher builds up a relationship of trust with his informants. Certainly, conventional statistical data, from the census or even from other people's survey work, will be of limited use here.

Deprivation

The problem of the inner city has popularly been seen as one of deprivation, and indeed it is this perception which is largely responsible for the visibility of inner city in recent public policy debates. However, we have not found this to be an area of crucial concern. Our review of the extensive literature on this subject has shown quite clearly that it has generally been regarded as an aspatial phenomenon requiring general policies. Forces contributing to individual and household deprivation are diverse, and many of them are covered in our examination of structural change described in the preceeding sections. The SSRC/DHSS project on transmitted deprivation — launched in 1974 and still ongoing — covers much of the rest of the field. What remains as a somewhat open question was the extent to which multiple deprivation exists among households and individuals — the only level at which it really has significance — as compared to areas, and whether deprivation is in the process of becoming more concentrated at the local level.

There have been a number of studies that have specifically sought to analyse social indicators at the micro scale in cities and conurbations, and some of this work has isolated parts of cities with particular concentrations of rather negative indicators. There have been only a very few studies — including those by Sally Holtermann, by Richard Berthoud, by the Department of the Environment (Holtermann, 1975; Berthoud, 1976; Department of the Environment 1975) — with a specific focus on the aspatial distribution of deprivation itself. In general these have not found evidence of very strong or systematic concentration, but they have all suffered from being based on census and similar information, and hence in having to make use of aggregate data (albeit at a spatially fine grain). Better understanding of deprivation will require longitudinal information about changes in circumstances over time, such as the birth of a child or the loss of a job. We need to understand how far such phenomena are concentrated either among particular socioeconomic groups or in particular geographical areas.

Some recent work, mainly in the United States, suggests that cities may be becoming more spatially differentiated: relatively prosperous, even very high-income areas may alternate with pockets of deprivation. Gentrification — an English word now borrowed by the Americans — may, it is suggested, be contributing to this process; so may polarisation resulting from continuing in-migration of deprived people, and differential out-migration of the more fortunate. This suggests another research avenue: the degree to which these spatial processes result in localities where it is difficult to provide families with adequate services. Still, as already suggested, it would be dangerous to approach this question save on the basis of figures disaggregated down to the level of the household.

Policy Responses

In recent years, inner city type policies — that is, spatially-oriented policies with special discrimination in favour of disadvantaged individuals in certain areas — have been competing for priority with quite different kinds of policy: some designated to attain general national objectives, such as national growth, or energy policy; some designed to help areas defined on a different basis, in particular assisted-area policies; and some designed to help identifiable individuals wherever they are found, generally on some defined criterion of need, such as welfare policies. No-one, in government or outside, has established any criteria for evaluating the effectiveness of these different policies. This is, of course, because of a number of evident difficulties: the fact that the precise effects of policies are very difficult to follow through because they are mixed up with the results of other policies, the lack of effective social indicators, and so on. Nevertheless, given the current crisis in public expenditure — a crisis that is in part independent of party political policies and reflects the poor prospects for economic growth — it appears an extremely important priority for research.

Insofar as area-based policies do prove to have some justification, another set of problems for research emerges. Very large amounts of public money have been sunk, in the last two decades of relative affluence and growth, into the physical reconstruction of the older parts of British cities and conurbations. Though they have displayed some common features (rebuilt central business districts, new housing in place of Victorian slums), nevertheless there are significant differences between one city and another. Some cities have rebuilt for the motor car, some not. Some have provided more commercial office space, some less. A few have provided new manufacturing capacity close to inner residential areas, others not. Linked to our study of 'success stories' in the late twentieth-century urban economy, we should be trying to study how far these different policy prescriptions have been successful in attracting new employment or retaining old jobs, whether for old or new residents, and how far they have attracted new residents, and whether or not this has been at the expense of the older inhabitants. Ideally, this would involve a close comparison of a number of the bigger conurbation cities to see how the local milieu has responded to massive physical change.

In discussing local labour markets, we have already suggested the need for a systematic study of recent governmental efforts in fields such as retraining, the supply of employment information, and mobility assistance. It seems to us that this should be a priority area for research.

Lastly, we badly needed an impartial assessment of the success — or otherwise — of community relations policies. We should look at the aspirations of ethnic groups — for housing, for jobs, for cultural identi-fication, for health and welfare provision — and ask how far official policies have met these aspirations. It might well be, for instance, that some of these groups have needs and priorities that are different from those of the majority of the host community. The existing Inner Area studies have suggested for instance that they may be more prone to set up their own businesses with quite limited capital, and more inclined to enter owner-occupation, even with the attendant disadvantage of what is often poorer housing, but that official policies — especially local authority ones — may run counter to those aspirations by destroying the supply of cheap older housing and low-cost workshop accom-modation, or by enforcing standards that are inappropriate. Though the Inner Area studies threw some light on such questions, much more work is needed.

Closely associated with these questions is another bundle, concerned with the pattern of local authority finance. We know enough about this to be sure that its impacts are inexplicit. The needs element of the rate support grant is a blunt instrument for compensating local authorities with heavy spending needs, while the resources element penalises those authorities seeking to augment their fiscal base. We have no way of saying, at present, either, on what basis and with what consequences is capital expenditure allocated between local authority areas, or whether the needs element is too generous or not generous enough in meeting the spending needs of the big cities. To try to examine that question would require new and better kinds of models that took account of national and local preferences, local costs of provision for given inputs, and scale and efficiency effects. There is a need too to look at the opportunities and constraints placed on local decision makers by specific grants and in particular by the partnership and programme arrangements. The biggest unknown, however, is how local authorities themselves allocate resources — both for capital and revenue expenditure — within their own areas, in response to the major changes we have identified. As suggested earlier in this report, too great an emphasis on the inner city or any other narrowly-defined spatial unit may deny resources to other people equally in need, while assisting some whose relative need is much less.

Inner city policies may take various forms — some centred on reviving the firm (and thereby assisting the entrepreneur), some centred on the plight of individual people, some more generally concerned with the quality of the entire environment. We need to develop research into the effectiveness and the impacts of these various policies. But in addition many other policies may be affecting inner cities — perhaps in different, even contrary directions. All this suggests the need to develop techniques of urban impact analysis similar to those now used for analysing urban problems in the United States. That programme of research, developed over the past year by the United States Department of Housing and Urban Development, systematically evaluates the effect of the whole range of governmental policies — not merely specific 'urban' policies, but also policies in other areas such as public sector employment, public sector purchases, or taxation — on the economic health and welfare of urban areas.

Overarching all these are more general questions — ones that are perhaps unanswerable, though we should start to try and tackle them, concerning the whole balance of social gains and losses resulting from the drift from the cities, and conversely the balance of costs and benefits that might result from policies to slow or stop the drift. There are clearly welfare gains as well as losses from decentralisation. Some operate at the level of the entire city region, some at the level of the inner city, some may be temporary and transitional, others more permanent. In the past, any general attempt to calculate a total economic balance sheet for alternative spatial distributions of people and economic activities, or for alternative paths of spatial development, has invariably proved too complex to tackle comprehensively and adequately. For that reason the Working Party does not include the topic in the select list of research proposals that follows.

Summary: Major Themes of the Research Programme

We now summarise those research topics, which after discussion we have selected from our work as most important and most promising for future study.

Structural change and the local economy

Under this head we should suggest a closely linked series of studies. First, deriving from the existing SSRC-funded work on macro-modelling of the economy, there would be an attempt to extend in depth the kind of medium-term scenario-writing essayed in Chapter 7. Following that, there would be in-depth studies of the adaptive capacities of different cities and regions faced with structural change, stressing particularly the contrast between successful adaptation and the lack of it. There would be a particular focus on the process of birth and early growth of small firms, and on the forces that aided or inhibited these processes. But there should also be work on the investment policies of larger firms, and on the relationship between these and the health of the small firms that might depend on larger corporations for orders. The studies should extend to the social and political milieu of different cities; in a later stage of the work, they should embrace international comparisons with cities on the European mainland.

Adjustment to the labour market

A second focus, loosely linked to the previous one, would be on the individual and his employment prospects within the local labour market. We would seek to focus here on those individuals most at risk — the unskilled, the young school leavers, the older worker — and to discover what constraints operated on their entry into the labour market. In particular, we would seek to examine commuting and migration as alternative solutions to extending the area of job search, and also to ask how far limited perceptions of the labour market provided a constraint. We would examine particularly the role of official agencies, such as the Manpower Services Commission, in advising seekers for work of job opportunities. Lastly, we would seek to evaluate the various programmes, developed particularly by the MSC, which have tried to up-grade the level of people's skills.

The relationship between the formal and informal economies

We believe that a promising approach would be to study in depth the relationship between the formal and informal sectors in one or more local case studies, considering individuals and their relationship to the two economies over time. This would link closely to the study of the birth and growth of small firms already suggested, and might indeed merge with it. We would want to focus particularly on the role of the informal sector in creating nascent firms, which might then enter the formal sector, and then later to see how this passage affected their chances of success. This would seem to demand the use of techniques of social anthropology, with intensive study based on a condition of trust between researcher and his subject.

We would hope too that this study, properly constructed, would throw light on the puzzling question of unemployment in the inner city economy. We suggest that the impact of unemployment may be quite different now from what it was thirty or forty years ago, because of the possibility of spending time — and generating income — within the informal economy. This again suggests that the immediate focus should once more be on the individual and his relation to the two economies.

Policy evaluation

Lastly, we recommend a series of studies that would seek to monitor the impact and effectiveness of public policy responses. The first stage of this would be a desk study, for each of our case studies, on the impact of public policy — not merely specifically 'urban' spatial policies but also aspatial ones — on the health and welfare of the particular cities concerned. Necessarily, such first-stage studies would be impressionistic, descriptive, and not particularly rigorous. They would however set the scene for a research programme on urban impact analysis, based on the important work recently produced in the United States, which might become a principal focus of a second-stage research programme.

Relating the Research Elements

The central problem is how to study these major research themes in depth, and how to interrelate them. Though we have rejected the inner city as such as a research focus, we remain convinced that the right approach is a spatially-based one: we want to examine, and to interrelate, these themes within the specific context of a limited number of contrasted local economies. For, central to our argument so far is the notion that the local milieu — a milieu that is not narrowly economic, and must also be understood through a study of local culture, psychology, politics and sociology — is the key to the relative success and failure of local economies. It follows also from our argument that we do not want to concentrate, as earlier studies have done, on local economic failure, but rather we want to devote considerable resources to looking at successful towns and regions. But since we intend to point out differences, we should be careful to choose examples of apparently unsuccessful as well as apparently successful regions, as well as those that may be in a state of transition. Lastly, though we reject the inner city as focus, we do not mean to exclude it from our attention. We wish, instead, to set it in the context of an entire local economy — one that may include suburbs and even exurban areas as well as the central business district and the archetypal inner city.

What we suggest, therefore, is a small set of limited local case studies, closely controlled from the centre so as to achieve maximum comparability of results. Though each study will have to achieve significant results in itself, that will not be the object of the exercise. The main point will be to draw comparative conclusions, and this will be the central theme of the book-length study that we propose as the final outcome of the research. The organisation of the research follows logically from this tension between local in-depth studies and the need for overall comparison. Each local study will necessarily be made by a different team, generally (but not inevitably) based on that local area. But the studies will be coordinated and even controlled from the centre.

The selection of the local case studies will be crucial to the success of the programme. As already said, each must embrace a local economic system. That is, each should be defined in terms of local labour market or travel-to-work area (or in some cases, a series of overlapping areas). So it is likely that each will go far beyond the boundaries of an inner city as conventionally defined, to include whole conurbations or cities and their surrounding spheres of influence — in other words their daily urban systems, as discussed in Chapter 2. In the case of a few larger conurbations, but especially in London, it will prove necessary to take only part of the entire urban area, probably on a sectoral basis.

Potential Case Study Areas and Research Centres

The first such case study should represent a classic example of a conurbation inner city suffering problems of structural economic decline, with long-term contraction of basic industries and an apparent failure to introduce sufficient new industry to compensate, coupled with a parallel failure of local entrepreneurship to generate new kinds of economic activity. The best known examples of such areas are Central Scotland, especially the Central Clydeside (Greater Glasgow or Strathclyde) conurbation, North East England, especially the Tyneside conurbation (Tyne and Wear Metropolitan County), and the Merseyside conurbation (Merseyside Metropolitan County). All these would be very strong candidates for study; the choice must depend upon the available research centres.

The second case study should logically concentrate on a conurbation in transition, with a long history of successful economic adaptation but with new emerging problems of decline of the basic industry, its repercussions on the whole economy, concentration on industrial ownership and control, and the apparent failure of an old small entrepreneurship tradition to generate new sources of economic growth. Here, there is only one choice: the West Midlands conurbation (West Midlands Metropolitan County).

The third case study should concentrate on an apparently successful and buoyant freestanding city with a good record of industrial adaptation in the twentieth century. The largest and most conspicuous among these appear to be Leicester, Nottingham and Bristol, while smaller centres include Southampton, Reading, and Norwich (though among these Reading should probably be considered in part as included in London's economic system). We believe that other things being equal, in order to gain the biggest advantage from comparability it would be right to choose one of the bigger — and also older — of these cities, preferably one that in purely physical terms appears to have a recognisable 'inner city', even an 'inner city problem'.

Finally, it is suggested that one study should be based on London. Here, however, because of the problem of size it will be necessary to choose sample areas. We propose that one such sample should be based on an area of apparently successful adaptation and full employment, another on a contrasting area that features decline of basic industries and highly localised unemployment. The obvious candidates for comparison are Outer West London (Hounslow, Hillingdon, Ealing), probably extending outwards to take in at least Slough and possibly Reading and Middle East London (Newham, Barking, Greenwich), concentrating on the docklands area.

We would again emphasise that the selection of the precise study areas should be done with great care. In many cases, as argued above, the appropriate area might be wide-ranging. Thus the problem conurbation (Clydeside, Tyneside, Merseyside) should range outwards to include the whole of the ring of new and expanded towns, with new implanted industry, outside the conurbation proper; similarly with the West Midlands example. The Bristol or East Midlands study should include a wide area of growing medium-sized towns within a 25—30-mile radius; while the London studies should look at the effect of outward movement of employment over a wide surrounding belt of the Outer Metropolitan Area. This will mean, especially in the London case, that each study will have to combine a broad-based descriptive overview and a series of in-depth studies. We return to this point below.

For each local case study, the basic theme would be an analysis of the capacity for structural change in the twentieth century, with a special focus on the period since 1950. A brief piece of desk research, using statistical and historical evidence, would provide a framework. Then, there would be a closer look at the pattern of births and deaths of firms and the impact of these on patterns of employment. This would be related to a study of the changing structure of employment and control of larger-scale industry. Interviews of selected firms would seek to establish the reasons for critical decisions to establish or close, expand or contract. There would be a special focus on the milieu within which the industrialist took his decisions — not merely the immediate economic milieu that includes items like the range and quality of the labour force and the availability of premises and transport facilities, but also the subtler social and political milieu affecting the climate of optimism or pessimism, and the capacity to innovate and take risks. Parallel to this, each study would look separately at the impact of structural change on the labour force, examining the patterns of adaptation in terms of job change, migration, commuting, unemployment, and entry into the formal economy.

The key to the successful conclusion of this work, however, does not lie merely in the completion of the four (or, counting London, five) case studies. Far more, it lies in their successful coordination through the production of common scenarios against which they will work; through refinement of their research briefs; through regular coordination during the period of the studies, at which concepts will be developed and results discussed and criticised; and finally, through production of the final report comparing and contrasting the results, and deriving from them conclusions of general relevance. The end result would not be a series of separate reports, but a major book-length study that looked, in greater detail than has been possible before, at the causes of urban growth and decline and at the responses of local individuals and institutions to both.

Such a programme, admittedly, omits other desirable and important subjects of research that have been raised in the previous discussion. One is the subject of international comparisons between British cities and cities on the European mainland that appear, so far, to have resisted the challenge of inner city decline. Another stands quite apart from the rest: it is the subject of urban impact analysis. We believe that quite apart from the research programme proposed here, it would be desirable to try to support research in these two fields in other ways.

Epilogue

The proposals in this chapter formed the burden of a report to the Research Board of the Social Science Research Council. Early in 1980 the Council approved a research budget of £275,000 over a three-year period to undertake this programme, under the control of an Executive Panel. The results of that research, to be published in the mid-1980s, will form an appropriate sequel to this present summary of the state of the art — against which, its findings may appropriately be judged.

Appendix

Published Papers of the SSRC Inner Cities Working Party

These have been published directly by the
Social Science Research Council,
1 Temple Avenue, London EC4
Inquiries should be addressed to
the Publications Officer.

1 *Understanding Land Values: A Review*
   By M. Edwards and D. Lovatt
2 *Changes in the Residential Populations of Inner Areas*
   By David Eversley and Lucy Bonnerjea
3 *Transport and the Inner City*
   By A.E. Gillespie
4 *Technological Change and the Inner City*
   By J.B. Goddard and A.T. Thwaites
5 *The Inner City Problem in Historical Context*
   By M. Hebbert
6 *Local Government Fiscal Problems: A Context for Inner Areas*
   By S. Kennett
7 *The Inner City in the Context of the Urban System*
   By Stephen Kennett
8 *The Inner City in the United States*
   By R. Kirwan
9 *Rural Development and its Relevance to the Inner City Debate*
   By M.J. Moseley
10 *Housing Market Processes and the Inner City*
   By A. Murie and R. Forrest
11 *Urban Governments and Economic Change*
   By K. Young, C. Mason and E. Mills

Bibliography

ABEL-SMITH, B., and TOWNSEND, P. (1965), *The Poor and the Poorest*. London: Bell.

ALLEN, G. C. (1976), *The British Disease: A Short Essay on the Nature and Causes of the Nation's Lagging Wealth* (Hobart Papers, 67). London: Institute of Economic Affairs.

AYODEJI, O., and VONK, F. (1980), *Metropolitan Employment Developments: An Inquiry into Some Aspects of Economic Change in the Larger City-Regions of the Netherlands*. Delft: Planologisch Studiecentrum T.N.O.

BEAUMONT, P. B. (1979). 'An Examination of Assisted Labour Mobility Policy' in MacLennan, D., and Parr J.B. (ed.), *Regional Policy: Past Experience and New Directions*. Oxford: Martin Robertson.

BELL, D. (1973), *The Coming of Post-Industrial Society: A Venture in Social Forecasting*. New York: Basic Books.

BENTHAM, C. G. (1978), 'Employment Problems of Male Unskilled Manual Workers in London: An Inner City Problem?', *Area*, 10, 158-60.

BERRY, B. J. L. (1970), 'The Geography of the United States in the Year 2000', *Transactions of the Institute of British Geographers*, 51, 21-53.

BERRY, B. J. L. (1976), 'The Counter-Urbanization Process: Urban America Since 1970' in Berry, B.J.L. (ed.), *Urbanization and Counter-Urbanization* (Sage Urban Affairs Annual Reviews, 11). Beverly Hills and London: Sage.

BERRY, B. J. L. (1980), 'Inner City Futures: An American Dilemma Revisited', *Transactions of the Institute of British Geographers, N.S.*, 5, 1-28.

BERRY, B. J. L. (forthcoming), 'Planning Metropolitan Areas Since World War Two' in Sutcliffe, A. (ed.). *Metropolis 1890-1940*. London: Mansell.

BERTHOUD, R. (1976), 'Where are London's Poor?', *Greater London Intelligence Quarterly*, 36, 5-12.

BIRCH, D. L. (1979), *The Job Generation Process* (M.I.T. Program on Neighborhood and Regional Change). Cambridge, Mass: Massachusetts Institute of Technology.

BONNAR, D. (1976), *Stochastic Models for Migration Analysis* (Geographical Papers, 51). Reading: University, Department of Geography.

BOOTH, C. (ed.) (1904), *Life and Labour of the People in London* (17 volumes in 3 series), London: Macmillan.

BRADLEY, J. E., KIRBY, A. M., and TAYLOR, P. J. (1978), 'Distance Decay and Dental Decay: A Study of Dental Health Among Primary School Children in Newcastle upon Tyne', *Regional Studies*, 12, 529-40.

BROADBENT, T. A. (1977), *Planning and Profit in the Urban Economy*. London: Methuen.

BURROWS, E. M. (1973), 'Office Employment and the Regional Problem', *Regional Studies*, 7, 17-31.

CAMERON, G. C. (1973), 'Intra-Urban Location and the New Plant', *Papers of the Regional Science Association*, 31, 125-43.

CHALKLEY, B. (1979), 'The Impact of Redevelopment on Displaced Industry'. Paper presented to the Institute of British Geographers, Annual Conference, Manchester. (Unpublished).

COMMISSION FOR RACIAL EQUALITY (1978), *Looking for Work: Black and White School Leavers in Lewisham*, London: CRE.

COMMITTEE ON SMALL FIRMS (1971), *Small Firms* (The 'Bolton' report), (Cmnd. 4811) London: H.M.S.O.

COMMUNITY DEVELOPMENT PROJECT (1977), *Gilding the Ghetto*. London/Newcastle: C.D.P.

CROFTON, B. (1975), 'Better Use of the Housing Stock', *Housing Review*, May-June, 73.

DAVIES, H. W. E. (1978), *The Inner City in Britain: Problems and Policies* (Tri-National Inner Cities Project, Working Paper). Reading: University, School of Planning Studies, (Unpublished).

DAVIES, H. W. E. (1980), *International Transfer and the Inner City: Report of the Tri-National Inner Cities Project* (University of Reading, School of Planning Studies Occasional Paper 5). Reading: University, School of Planning Studies. (Mimeo).

DEAKIN, N. and UNGERSON, C. (1977), *Leaving London: Planned Mobility and the Inner City*. London: Heinemann Educational Books, for Centre for Environmental Studies.

DEPARTMENT OF EDUCATION AND SCIENCE (1972), *Educational Priority, Vol. 1. E.P.A. Problems and Policies* (By A.H. Halsey). London: H.M.S.O.

DEPARTMENT OF THE ENVIRONMENT (1972), *New Local Authorities: Management and Structure*, London: H.M.S.O.

DEPARTMENT OF THE ENVIRONMENT (1975), *Study of the Inner Areas of Conurbations, Vol. 1, Summary and Conclusions; Vol. 2, Detailed Studies*. London: D.o.E.

DEPARTMENT OF THE ENVIRONMENT (1977a), *Inner Area Studies: Liverpool, Birmingham, and Lambeth: Summary of Consultants' Final Reports*. London: H.M.S.O.

DEPARTMENT OF THE ENVIRONMENT (1977b), *Policy for the Inner Cities*. London: H.M.S.O.

DEPARTMENT OF THE ENVIRONMENT (1977c), *Change or Decay: Final Report of the Liverpool Inner Area Study*. London: H.M.S.O.

DEPARTMENT OF THE ENVIRONMENT (1977d), *Unequal City: Final Report of the Birmingham Inner Area Study*. London: H.M.S.O.

DEPARTMENT OF THE ENVIRONMENT (1977e), *Recreation and Deprivation in Inner Urban Areas*. London: H.M.S.O.

DICKEN, P. and LLOYD, P. E. (1979), 'The Corporate Dimension of Employment Change in the Inner City' in Jones, C. (ed.), *Urban Deprivation and the Inner City*. London: Croom Helm.

DONNISON, D. and EVERSLEY, D. E. C. (1973), *London: Urban Patterns, Problems and Policies*, London: Heinemann Educational Books.

DONNISON, D. and SOTO, P. (1980), *The Good City: A Study of Urban Development and Policy in Britain*. London: Heinemann Educational Books.

EDWARDS, J. and BATLEY, R. (1978), *The Politics of Positive Discrimination: An Evaluation of the Urban Programme 1967-77*. London: Tavistock.

EDWARDS, M. and LOVATT, D. (1980), *Understanding Urban Land Values: A Review* (The Inner City in Context, Paper 1). London: Social Science Research Council.

EVERSLEY, D. E. C. (1973), *The Planner in Society: The Changing Role of a Profession*. London: Faber and Faber.

EVERSLEY, D. E. C. (1975), 'Searching for London's Lost Soul; or How not to Get from There and Then to Here and Now', *The London Journal*, 1, 103-17.

EVERSLEY, D. E. C. (1978), 'The Falling Birth Rate — Implications of Urban or Regional Planning' in Grime, K. (ed.), *Social Trends in City and Regional Planning* (Regional Studies Association, Discussion Paper 10). London: Regional Studies Association.

EVERSLEY, D. and BONNERJEA, L. (1980), *Changes in the Resident Population of Inner Areas* (The Inner City in Context, Paper 2). London: Social Science Research Council.

EVERSLEY, D. E. C. (forthcoming), 'Threats to the Survival of the Metropolis: The View from 1980' in Sutcliffe, A. (ed.), *Metropolis 1890-1940*. London: Mansell.

FOSTER, C. (1977) 'Central Government's Response to the Layfield Report', *CIPFA Conference, Eastbourne (CES-PSI)*. London: Centre for Environmental Studies.

FOTHERGILL, S. and GUDGIN, G. (1979), 'Regional Employment Change: A Sub-Regional Explanation', *Progress in Planning*, **12**, 155-219.

FREEMAN, C. and JAHODA, M. (1978), *World Futures: The Great Debate*. Oxford: Martin Robertson.

FROST, M. and SPENCE, N. (1978), *Industrial and Occupational Change in British Sub-Regions, 1966-71* (Working Paper 3, Urban and Regional Unemployment in Britain). London: London School of Economics and King's College, London.

GANS, H. (1971), 'Poverty and Culture: Some Basic Questions about Methods of Studying Life-Styles of the Poor', in Townsend, P. (ed.), *The Concept of Poverty*. London: Heinemann Educational Books, 146-64.

GILJE, E. (1975), *Migration Patterns in and Around London* (Research Memorandum, 470). London: Greater London Council.

GILLESPIE, A. E. (1980), *Transport and the Inner City* (The Inner City in Context, Paper 3). London: Social Science Research Council.

GLICKMAN, N. J. (1978), *The Growth and Management of the Japanese Urban System*. New York: Academic Press.

GLICKMAN, N. J. (ed.) (1980), *The Urban Impacts of Federal Policies*. Baltimore: Johns Hopkins University Press.

GLICKMAN, N. J. (ed.) (1981), Urban Impact Analysis. Special Issue, Built Environment, 6, no. 2.

GODDARD, J. B. (1978), 'Office Location and Urban and Regional Development in Britain', in Daniels, P.W. (ed.), *Spatial Patterns of Office Growth and Location*. Chichester: John Wiley.

GODDARD, J. B. and SPENCE, N. A. (1976). 'A National Perspective on Employment Changes in Urban Labour Markets and Questions about the Future of the Provincial Conurbations'. Paper presented to Centre for Environmental Studies Conference on Employment in the Inner City, University of York.

GODDARD. J. B. and SMITH, W. (1978), 'Changes in Corporate Control in the British Urban System, 1972-77' *Environment and Planning, A*, **10**, 1073-84.

GODDARD, J. B. and THWAITES, A. T. (1980), *Technological Change and the Inner City* (The Inner City in Context, Paper 4). London: Social Science Research Council.

GOULD, T. and LACY, S. (1973), 'A Note on Migration and Commuting in the South East Region: 1965-66', *Greater London Council Intelligence Quarterly Bulletin*, **25**, 63-5.

HALL, P. (1977a), *Europe 2000*. London: Duckworth.

HALL, P. (1977b), *Green Fields and Grey Areas* (proceedings of Royal

Town Planning Institute Annual Conference, Chester). London: Royal Town Planning Institute.

HALL, P. (1978), 'Spending Priorities in the Inner City', *New Society*, 46, 698-9.

HALL, P. (1980a), 'Two Nations or One? The Geography of Deprivation', *New Society*, 51, 331-3.

HALL, P. (1980b), 'New Trends in European Urbanization', *The Annals of the American Academy of Political and Social Science*, 451, 45-51.

HALL, P. and HAY, D. (1980), *Growth Centres in the European Urban System*, London: Heinemann Educational Books.

HAMBLETON, R. (1977), 'Policies for Areas', *Local Government Studies, New Series*, 3, no. 2, 13-29.

HAMNETT, C. (1976a), 'Social Change and Social Segregation in Inner London 1961-71'. *Urban Studies*, 13, 261-72.

HAMNETT, C. (1976b), *Multiple Deprivation in the Inner City* (Unit 15 in Open University course 'Patterns of Inequality'). Milton Keynes: Open University Press.

HARRIS, D. F. and TAYLOR, F. J. (1978), *The Service Sector: its Changing Role as a Source of Employment* (Centre for Environmental studies, C.E.S. Research Series 25). London: Centre for Environmental Studies.

HARRISON, A. J. and WHITEHEAD, C. (1978), 'Is there an Inner City Problem?, *Three Banks Review*, September, 31-45.

HEBBERT, M. (1980), *The Inner City Problem in Historical Context* (The Inner City in Context, Paper 5). London: Social Science Research Council.

HIGGENS, J. (1978), *The Poverty Business*. Oxford: Blackwell.

HOLTERMANN, S. (1975), 'Areas of Urban Deprivation in Great Britain: An Analysis of 1971 Census Data', *Social Trends*, H.M.S.O., 6, 33-47.

HOLTERMANN, S. (1978), 'The Welfare Economics of Priority Area Policies', *Journal of Social Policy*, 7, 23-40.

IMBER, V. (1977), *A Classification of the English Personal Social Service Authorities* (Department of Health and Social Security, Statistical and Research Report Series, 16). London: H.M.S.O.

JENKINS, C. and SHERMAN, B. (1979), *The Collapse of Work*. London: Eyre Methuen.

JOHNSON, J. H. and SALT, J. (1978), 'Labour Migration Policies in Great Britain'. Paper presented at Institute of British Geographers Population Geography Study Group Conference on Population Policies, University of Durham. (Unpublished).

JOHNSON, J., SALT, J., and WOOD, P. (1974), *Housing and the Migration of Labour in England and Wales*. Farnborough: Saxon House.

JONES, C. (1979), 'Population Decline in Cities' in Jones, C. (ed.), *Urban Deprivation and the Inner City*. London: Croom Helm.

JONES, T. P. and McEVOY, D. (1978), 'Race and Space in Cloud-Cuckoo Land', *Area*, **10**, 162-6.

JOSEPH, K. (1972), 'The Cycle of Deprivation' in *Playgroups in Education and the Social Services*, London: Pre-school Playgroups Association.

JOSEPH, K. (1979), 'The Class War' (An edited extract from the Gilbreth lecture). *The Guardian*, July 18, 7.

KARN, V. (1979), 'Low Income Owner Occupation in the Inner City', in Jones, C. (ed.), *Urban Deprivation and the Inner City*. London: Croom Helm.

KEEBLE, D. E. (1976), *Industrial Location and Planning in the United Kingdom*. London: Methuen.

KEEBLE, D. E. (1980), 'Industrial Decline, Regional Policy, and the Urban-Rural Manufacturing Shift in the United Kingdom', *Environment and Planning*, A, **12**, 945-62.

KENNETT, S. (1978), 'Differential Migration between British Labour Markets; Some Policy Implications'. Paper presented to the Population Study Group (Institute of British Geographers), Durham.

KENNETT, S. (1980a), *The Inner City in the Context of the Urban System* (The Inner City in Context, Paper 7). London: Social Science Research Council.

KENNETT, S. (1980b), *Local Government Fiscal Problems: A Context for Inner Areas* (The Inner City in Context, Paper 6). London: Social Science Research Council.

KENNETT, S. and SPENCE, N. (1979), 'British Population Trends in the 1970s', *Town and Country Planning*, **48**, 7.

KINCAID, J. A. (1973), *Poverty and Equality in Britain*. Harmondsworth: Penguin Books.

KIRBY, A. (1978), *The Inner City: Causes and Effects*. Corbridge: Retailing and Planning Associates.

KIRWAN, R. M. (1980a), *The Inner City in the United States* (The Inner City in Context, Paper 8). London: Social Science Research Council.

KIRWAN, R. M. (1980b), 'The Fiscal Context' in Cameron, G. (ed.), *The Future of the British Conurbations: Policies and Prescriptions for Change*. London: Longman.

KOCH, R. (1980), '»Counterurbanisation« auch in Westeuropa?' *Informationen zur Raumentwicklung, 1980*, 59-69.

KONDRATIEFF, N. D. (1935 (1925)), 'The Long Waves in Economic Life', *The Review of Economic Statistics*, **17**, 105-15.

LANSLEY, S. (1979) 'Rate Support Grant and the Inner Cities', *CES Review*, **6**, 56-63.

LAWLESS, P. (1979), *Urban Deprivation and Government Initiative*. London: Faber.

LEIGH, R. and NORTH, D. (1978), 'Regional Aspects of Acquisition Activity in british Manufacturing Industry', *Regional Studies*, 12, 227-246.

LEONARD, S. (1979), 'Accessibility and Eligibility Constraints in Industrial Training: The Case of Greater London' (Geography Department, Working Note 8.) London: London School of Economics.

LEWIS, O. (1961), *The Children of Sanchez*. New York: Random House.

LUPSHA, P. A. and SIEMBIEDA, W. J. (1977), 'The Poverty of Public Services in the Land of Plenty: An Analysis and Interpretation' in Petty, D. C. and Watkins, A. J. (eds.), *The Rise of the Sunbelt Cities* (Urban Affairs Annual Reviews 14), 169-90. Beverly Hills and London: Sage.

McALLISTER, I., PARRY, R., and ROSE, R. (1979), *United Kingdom Rankings: The Territorial Dimension in Social Indicators* (Studies in Public Policy, 44). Glasgow: Strathclyde University, Centre for the Study of Public Policy.

McCARTHY, K. F. and MORRISON, P. A. (1977), 'The Changing Demographic and Economic Structure of Non-Metropolitan Areas in the United States', *International Regional Science Review*, 2, 123-42.

McCARTHY, K. F. and MORRISON, P. A. (1979), *The Changing Demographic and Economic Structure of Non-Metropolitan Areas in the United States* (R-2399-EDA). Santa Monica: RAND Corporation. (Mimeo).

McDERMOTT, P. J. (1978), 'Changing Manufacturing Enterprise in the Metropolitan Environment: The Case of Electronics in London', *Regional Studies*, 12, 541-50.

McGREGOR, A. (1980), *Urban Unemployment: A Study of Differential Unemployment Rates in Glasgow* (CRU Papers). Edinburgh: Scottish Office, Central Research Unit.

McKAY, D. H., and COX, A. W. (1979a), *The Politics of Urban Change*. London: Croom Helm.

McKAY, D. and COX, A. (1979b), 'Confusion and Reality in Public Policy: The Case of the British Urban Programme' in Open University, Politics, People and Administration Course Team, *Public Policy in Theory and Practice*. London: Hodder and Stoughton.

MASSEY, D. B. (1976), *Restructuring and Regionalism: Some Spatial Implications for the Crisis in the U.K.* (C.E.S. WN 449). London: Centre for Environmental Studies.

MASSEY, D. B. and MEEGAN, R. A. (1978), 'Industrial Restructuring versus the Cities', *Urban Studies*, 15, 273-88.

MASSEY, D. B., and MEEGAN, R. A. (1979), 'The Geography of Industrial Reorganisation: The Spatial Effects of the Restructuring of the Electrical Engineering Sector under the Industrial Reorganisation Corporation', *Progress in Planning*, 10, Part 3, 155-237.

MINISTRY OF HOUSING AND LOCAL GOVERNMENT (1968), *Old Houses into New Homes*. London: H.M.S.O.

MINISTRY OF HOUSING AND LOCAL GOVERNMENT (1969), *People and Planning: Report of the Committee on Public Participation in Planning*. (The 'Skeffington' Report). London: H.M.S.O.

MOYNIHAN, D. (1966), 'What is Community Action?', *The Public Interest*, 5, Fall, 3-8.

MURIE, A. and FORREST, R. (1980), *Housing Market Processes and the Inner City* (The Inner City in Context, Paper 10). London: Social Science Research Council.

NABARRO, R. and McDONALD I. (1978), 'The Urban Programme: Will It Really Help the Inner City?', *The Planner*, 64, 171-3.

OECD (Organisation for Economic Cooperation and Development) (1979), *Interfutures: Final Report: Mastering the Probable and Managing the Unpredictable*. Paris: OECD.

OVERTON, E. (1980) 'The Fertility of the Population of New Commonwealth and Pakistani Ethnic Origin: Some Recent Estimates', *Policy Studies*, 1, 53-64.

PAHL, R. (1978), 'Will the Inner City Problem Ever Go Away?', *New Society*, 45, 678-81.

PAHL, R. and GERSHUNY, J. (1980), 'Britain in the Decade of the Three Economies', *New Society*, 51, 7-9.

PALMER, D. and GLEAVE, D. (1978), 'Moving to Find Work', *New Society*, 45, 454.

PERMAN, R. and MOORE, P. (1975), *Models of Residential Mobility in London* (Research Memorandum, 544). London: Greater London Council.

PERRY, D. and WATKINS, A. (1978), *The Rise of the Sunbelt Cities*. (Urban Affairs Annual Reviews, 14). Beverly Hills and London: Sage.

PIVEN, F. (1974), 'The Great Society: Moderating Disorder in the Ghettos' in Cloward, R. and F. Piven, *The Politics of Turmoil*. New York: Pantheon Books.

PRYCE, K. (1979), 'Hustlers, Teenyboppers and Other Sinners', *New Society*, 47, 727-30.

REID, G. L. (1976), 'Manpower Policy and the Inner Cities' in Evans, A., and Eversley, D. E. C. (eds.), *The Inner City: Employment and Industry*. London: Heinemann Educational Books.

ROSTOW, W. W. (1977), 'Regional Change in the Fifth Kondratieff Upswing' in Perry, D. C. and Watkins, A. J. (eds.), *The Rise of the Sunbelt Cities* (Urban Affairs Annual Reviews, 14), 83-103. Beverly hills and London: Sage.

ROYAL COMMISSION ON THE DISTRIBUTION OF INCOME AND WEALTH (1978), Report No. 6. *Lower Incomes*, (Cmnd. 7175). London: H.M.S.O.

SHARP, M. (1980), 'Technology and Growth: The Challenge of Long-Term Structural Change', *Futures*, 12, 370-85.

SHEPHERD, J., WESTAWAY, J., and LEE, T. (1974), *A Social Atlas of London*. Oxford: Clarendon.

SMITH, D. J. (1977), *Racial Disadvantage in Britain: the PEP Report*. Harmondsworth: Penguin Books.

SMITH, D. M. (1979), *Where the Grass is Greener: Living in an Unequal World*. Harmondsworth: Penguin Books.

SMITH, I. J. (1979), 'The Effect of External Takeovers on Manufacturing Employment Change in the Northern Region between 1963 and 1973', *Regional Studies*, 13, 421-37.

STEWART, M. and UNDERWOOD, J. (1980), *Inner City Policy in England: Some Preliminary Thoughts on Organisational Form and Central/Local Relations*. Bristol: School for Advanced Urban Studies.

THOMAS, C. and WINYARD, S. (1979), 'Rural Incomes' in Shaw, J.M. (ed.), *Rural Deprivation and Planning*. Norwich: Geo Abstracts.

THRIFT, N. J. (1979), 'Unemployment in the Inner City: Urban Problem or Structural Imperative? A Review of the British Experience' in Hobart, D. T. and Johnston R. J. (eds.), *Geography and the Urban Environment*, vol. 2. Chichester: John Wiley.

TOWNSEND, P. (1976), 'Area Deprivation Policies', *New Statesman*, 12, 168-71.

TOWNSEND, P. (1979), *Poverty in the United Kingdom: A Survey of Household Resources and Standard of Living*. Harmondsworth: Penguin Books.

U. S. NATIONAL RESOURCES PLANNING BOARD (1937), *Our Cities: Their Role in the National Economy*. Washington D.C.: Government Printing Office.

VALE, G. R. (1971), *Is the Housing Problem Solved? A Review of Recent Estimates*. London: Housing Centre Trust.

VINING, D. R. (1981), 'Recent Dispersal from the World's Industrial Core Regions' in Kawashima, T. (ed.), *Urbanization Processes: Experiences of Eastern and Western Countries*. Oxford: Pergamon.

VINING, D. R. and KONTULY, T. (1977), 'Increasing Returns to City Size in the Face of an Impending Decline in the Size of Large Cities: Which is the Bogus Fact?', *Environment and Planning*, A, 9, 59-62.

VINING, D. R. and STRAUSS A. (1977), 'A Demonstration that the Current Deconcentration of Population in the United States is a Clean Break with the Past', *Environment and Planning, A*, 9, 751-8.

WEBBER, R. J. (1975), *Liverpool Social Area Study: 1971 Data: Final Report* (PRAG Technical Papers, TP 14). London: Centre for Environmental Studies, Planning Research Applications Group.

WEBSTER, D. (1978), 'Regional Housing Strategies: Changing Problems and Changing Responses' in Grime, K., *Social Trends in City and*

Regional Planning (Regional Studies Association Discussion Paper, 10). London: Regional Studies Association. (Mimeo).

WICK, M. (1977), 'Social Policy for the Inner Cities' in Brown, M. and Baldwin M. (eds.). *The Year Book of Social Policy in Britain 1977*. London and Henley: Routledge and Kegan Paul.

WILLMOTT, P. (1980), 'The Social Causes of Inner City Decline', *Proceedings of the British Association for the Advancement of Science 1980, Section N*. (Mimeo).

Index